LegalWay's Winning Child Custody Battle for Fathers

Success Strategies for Dads to Secure Custody and Protect their Parental Rights

Lilian Justus

Copyright © 2024 Lilian Justus

All Rights Reserved

This guide is for informational purposes only. The author and publisher are not liable for any damages or injuries resulting from the use of the information provided. Always consult a professional for specific advice and follow safety guidelines when undertaking any such projects.

Table of Contents

LegalWay's Winning Child Custody Battle for Fathers i

Table of Contents iii

Introduction 1

Chapter 1: Understanding Custody Laws 8

    Types of Custody: Legal vs. Physical 9

    Common Custody Terms and Definitions ... 15

    State-Specific Custody Regulations 23

Chapter 2: Assessing Your Situation 31

    Evaluating Your Parental Role and Contributions 32

    Recognizing Potential Custody Challenges . 39

    Identifying the Child's Best Interests 48

Chapter 3: Preparing Essential Documentation 57

    Collecting Proof of Parenting Involvement 58

    Organizing Financial and Employment Records 67

Gathering Communication and Co-Parenting Logs 77

Chapter 4: Building a Strong Case 88

Creating a Detailed Parenting Plan............. 89

Understanding What Judges Look For 99

Avoiding Common Mistakes 109

Chapter 5: Hiring the Right Legal Support ... 118

Choosing an Experienced Custody Lawyer 119

Communicating Effectively with Your Attorney 128

Managing Legal Costs 137

Chapter 6: Navigating Court Procedures 147

Filing the Initial Custody Petition 148

Preparing for Custody Hearings 156

Presenting Evidence and Witnesses 165

Chapter 7: Handling Mediation and Negotiation 174

Preparing for Mediation Sessions.............. 175

Negotiating Custody and Visitation Agreements 182

Chapter 8: Ensuring a Positive Image 199

Maintaining Good Behavior During the Custody Process 200

Managing Social Media and Public Perception 209

Addressing Allegations and Misunderstandings 218

Chapter 9: Supporting Your Child During the Process 227

Communicating the Situation to Your Child 228

Prioritizing Emotional and Mental Well-Being 235

Maintaining Consistent Parenting Practices 244

Chapter 10: Finalizing Custody and Moving Forward 252

Understanding Custody Orders and Compliance 253
Preparing for Post-Judgment Modifications 260
Co-Parenting Strategies for Long-Term Success 267
Conclusion 276

Introduction

Fighting for custody of your child is one of the most emotionally charged and life-changing battles you may ever face. It's a journey filled with highs that leave you breathless with hope and lows that can break even the strongest spirit. The joy of imagining a future where you can be the present, nurturing parent your child deserves collides with the frustration of navigating a legal system that often feels daunting and overwhelming. Yet, here you are, determined to do what's right—not just for yourself but for the little one who depends on you.

This book, **_LegalWay's Winning Child Custody Battle for Fathers_**, is designed to be the guiding light in what may feel like a never-ending storm. It's a place where knowledge meets strategy and emotion meets reassurance. You are not alone. Thousands of fathers have stood where you are now—uncertain, determined, and searching for answers. They've felt the weight of stereotypes and the sting of doubt, yet they've emerged victorious. You can too.

Custody battles often evoke a rollercoaster of emotions. The initial realization that you may need to fight for your role as a parent can feel like a punch to the gut. The thought of proving your worthiness to strangers in a courtroom can stir up feelings of fear, anger, and even despair. But these feelings are natural, and they don't define you. Instead, they reflect the depth of your love and commitment to your child. Emotions are powerful, but they're also fleeting. Knowledge, on the other hand, is enduring. And knowledge is what this book is all about.

There's no denying that the custody process is riddled with challenges. Perhaps you've been told that the legal system is stacked against fathers or that your chances of winning are slim. Maybe you're worried about the financial toll or the personal sacrifices required. These concerns are valid, but they are not insurmountable. This book doesn't shy away from these realities. Instead, it equips you with tools and strategies to confront them head-on.

Every father who embarks on this journey faces a unique set of struggles. Some wrestle with the misconception that fathers are less capable caregivers. Others face barriers such as demanding work schedules, strained co-parenting relationships, or past mistakes being unfairly scrutinized. But no matter your situation, this book will help you evaluate your strengths, address your challenges, and build a case that highlights your value as a parent.

Despite the struggles, there are moments of triumph and joy along the way. The first time you create a detailed parenting plan that showcases your dedication, you'll feel a surge of confidence. When you see the evidence of your involvement as a father laid out in an organized, compelling way, you'll know you're making progress. And when you witness your child thriving because of your love and effort, you'll understand that every step of this process is worth it.

This book celebrates those highs. It reminds you that the custody battle isn't just about winning a legal case; it's about securing your place in your child's life. It's about creating a future where your child knows, without a shadow of a doubt, that they are loved, supported, and cherished by their father.

Here, you'll find a comprehensive roadmap that demystifies the custody process. From understanding legal terms to preparing documentation, from presenting yourself effectively in court to handling mediation with grace—this book covers it all. Each chapter is filled with actionable advice, practical tips, and real-life examples that will make the journey less intimidating and more manageable.

But this isn't just a manual; it's a source of assurance. The custody process is complex, but you don't need to navigate it alone or unprepared. By understanding what to expect and how to respond, you'll feel more confident and empowered at every step.

While no one can guarantee outcomes, preparation and persistence are your greatest allies. This book will show you how to position yourself as the best possible parent in the eyes of the court. It will help you focus on what truly matters—the well-being of your child—and demonstrate that commitment through every action you take.

The custody battle isn't a sprint; it's a marathon. There will be setbacks and moments of doubt, but every step forward is progress. Every document you gather, every argument you refine, and every mediation session you attend is a testament to your dedication. This book will remind you that even when the road feels long, you are moving closer to the goal.

Above all, this book offers hope. Hope that you can overcome the obstacles ahead. Hope that the bond you share with your child will shine through, even in the face of adversity. Hope that, at the end of this process, you'll emerge not only as a father but as an advocate for your child's best interests.

Hope is powerful because it fuels action. It transforms fear into determination and doubt into resolve. With every page you turn, let that hope grow. Let it remind you why you're fighting and who you're fighting for.

You've taken the first step simply by opening this book. Now, take the next step: start reading.

Each chapter is a building block, designed to strengthen your case and clarify your path forward. Don't rush through; absorb the information, reflect on how it applies to your situation, and take action.

The journey ahead may not be easy, but it is worth it. For every challenge you face, this book is here to guide you. For every doubt you feel, this book is here to reassure you. And for every victory, big or small, this book is here to celebrate with you.

Your child deserves a father who is present, loving, and involved. You deserve the chance to be that father without barriers or limitations. Together, let's make it happen. Turn the page, and let's get started.

Chapter 1: Understanding Custody Laws

Custody laws define the legal rights and responsibilities of parents concerning their children after separation or divorce. Understanding these laws is essential for navigating the custody process and protecting your parental rights. Familiarity with key terms and legal principles ensures you can make informed decisions that support your child's well-being.

Types of Custody: Legal vs. Physical

When fathers like you are preparing for a custody case, understanding the basics of legal and physical custody is crucial. This knowledge helps you clarify what's at stake and allows you to make informed decisions about your child's well-being. Each type of custody carries unique responsibilities and implications, so let's break them down in detail.

Legal Custody: Making Decisions for Your Child

Legal custody refers to the authority to make important decisions about your child's life. This includes areas like education, healthcare, religious upbringing, and general welfare. Courts recognize that these decisions significantly shape a child's future, and they aim to grant this authority in a way that best serves the child's interests.

- **Sole Legal Custody:** One parent has the exclusive right to make major decisions for the child. This may happen if the court determines that one parent is unfit or less involved in the child's life.
- **Joint Legal Custody:** Both parents share decision-making authority. This arrangement requires good communication and cooperation between parents, as they'll need to agree on major choices for the child.

For fathers aiming to secure legal custody, showing the court your involvement in your child's life is key. Document instances where you've made impactful decisions—like enrolling your child in school, taking them to doctor's appointments, or being actively involved in their extracurricular activities.

Physical Custody: Where Your Child Lives

Physical custody determines where your child lives and who provides their daily care. It directly impacts the day-to-day parenting responsibilities and routines.

- **Sole Physical Custody:** The child lives primarily with one parent, while the other parent may have visitation rights. This arrangement is common if one parent's home environment is deemed more stable or suitable.
- **Joint Physical Custody:** The child spends significant time with both parents, often splitting weeks, months, or holidays. This arrangement works well when both parents live close to each other and can maintain a consistent schedule.

If you're seeking physical custody, it's essential to demonstrate that your home is a safe, nurturing environment. Courts often look at factors such as your living situation, proximity to the child's school, and your ability to provide a stable routine.

How Courts Decide Custody

Courts prioritize the child's best interests in custody decisions. This means they'll assess various factors, including:

- The relationship between each parent and the child.
- Each parent's ability to meet the child's emotional, physical, and educational needs.
- The child's preferences, depending on their age and maturity.
- Any history of abuse, neglect, or substance issues.

As a father, it is essential that you demonstrate to the court that you are a responsible, committed, and nurturing parent who prioritizes your child's well-being above all else. The court will be evaluating not only your ability to meet your child's physical needs but also your emotional and psychological support.

Tips for Fathers Navigating Custody Decisions

1. Stay Involved

Attend parent-teacher conferences, extracurricular activities, and medical appointments. Courts value engaged parents.

2. Communicate Respectfully

Work towards a cooperative relationship with the other parent, as it reflects your ability to co-parent effectively.

3. Organize Your Records

Maintain documentation of your involvement, including emails, texts, or schedules that show your active role in the child's life.

4. Consult Legal Help

Consider enlisting the help of an attorney who specializes in father's rights or custody cases to ensure that you build the strongest possible case for your child's custody. A lawyer with experience in this specific area will be well-versed in the legal nuances and challenges that fathers often face in custody battles.

Strategic Suggestions

- Focus on demonstrating your commitment through actions, not just words. Volunteer for tasks like taking your child to appointments or helping with homework.
- Always prioritize your child's needs over conflicts with the other parent. Courts are impressed by fathers who show maturity and an unwavering focus on their child's well-being.
- Be consistent in your parenting role. Courts prefer to see a stable, reliable presence in a child's life.

Understanding the difference between legal and physical custody is a foundational step in custody cases. With this clarity, you're better prepared to advocate for your rights as a father and prioritize your child's best interests.

Common Custody Terms and Definitions

When stepping into a custody case, the terms used in court and legal documents can feel overwhelming. Understanding these terms is critical to ensuring you're fully prepared and can advocate for your rights and your child's best interests. This section explains the most commonly used custody terms, so you can navigate the process confidently.

Primary Custody Terms

Custody discussions revolve around the two main types of custody: legal custody and physical custody. Let's look at some key terms often tied to these concepts.

1. Custodial Parent

This refers to the parent who has physical custody of the child for the majority of the time. They are responsible for the child's day-to-day care.

2. Non-Custodial Parent

This is the parent who doesn't have primary physical custody but may have visitation rights or scheduled parenting time.

3. Sole Custody

When one parent has exclusive rights to either legal or physical custody, or both. This is usually granted if the other parent is deemed unable to fulfill their parenting responsibilities.

4. Joint Custody

This involves both parents sharing rights and responsibilities for the child. Joint custody can apply to legal custody, physical custody, or both.

Parenting Time and Visitation

The terms surrounding visitation and shared time with your child can often be confusing. There are many factors that determine the arrangement, including the specific language used to describe how time with your child is allocated between you and the other parent. Here are some definitions to keep in mind:

1. Parenting Time

This refers to the schedule established by the court outlining when the child spends time with each parent.

2. Supervised Visitation

When a neutral third party oversees a parent's time with their child. Courts often impose this when there are concerns about the child's safety.

3. Unsupervised Visitation

Regular visitation where the non-custodial parent can spend time with the child without supervision. As a father, demonstrating that you can handle unsupervised parenting time responsibly is critical in custody cases.

Other Important Custody-Related Terms

To navigate custody battles, you'll also encounter these terms:

1. Best Interests of the Child

This is the standard courts use to decide custody arrangements. It encompasses the child's emotional, physical, and developmental needs.

2. Parental Alienation

When one parent attempts to turn the child against the other parent through manipulation or badmouthing. Courts take allegations of parental alienation seriously.

3. Parenting Plan

A formal agreement between parents outlining custody, visitation schedules, and decision-making responsibilities. A well-prepared parenting plan can prevent conflicts and show the court you are proactive.

4. Modification

This is a request to change an existing custody order due to a significant change in circumstances. For example, a parent relocating or experiencing a change in work schedule might prompt a modification request.

Common Custody Misconceptions

It's important to clear up a few myths about custody:

Myth #1: Courts always favor mothers.

Fact: Most courts now evaluate cases based on the child's best interests and not gender. Fathers who demonstrate involvement and capability have a strong chance of gaining custody.

Myth #2: Joint custody means a 50/50 time split.

Fact: Joint custody doesn't always mean equal time. Courts consider what works best for the child's schedule and stability.

How These Terms Affect Your Case

Understanding these terms not only makes the legal process less intimidating but also allows you to advocate for your rights effectively. For example:

- Knowing what "best interests of the child" entails helps you prepare evidence of your positive parenting.
- Understanding "parenting plans" allows you to create a comprehensive and practical proposal for custody arrangements.
- Recognizing terms like "modification" ensures you can adjust custody agreements when needed.

Tips for Mastering Custody Terminology

1. Research Local Terms

Some states have unique definitions or additional terms, so check your state's custody laws.

2. Stay Organized

Use custody terms when communicating with your attorney or presenting evidence to the court. This shows professionalism and preparedness.

3. **Avoid Jargon in Personal Conversations**

While understanding legal terms is crucial, communicate in simple terms when talking to your child or co-parent to avoid confusion.

Strategic Suggestions

- Use custody terms accurately when documenting or discussing your parenting role. For instance, refer to time spent with your child as "parenting time" rather than simply "visitation."
- Draft a detailed parenting plan that uses proper terminology while emphasizing your willingness to cooperate for the child's benefit.
- Prepare to explain how you meet the "best interests of the child" standard during court proceedings.

Mastering these custody terms and definitions gives you a firm foundation to navigate your custody case successfully. Clear communication and understanding of these terms show the court that you're knowledgeable and ready to prioritize your child's well-being.

State-Specific Custody Regulations

When preparing for a custody battle, understanding the custody laws and regulations specific to your state is essential. Each state has its own legal framework governing custody decisions, including factors courts consider, the terminology used, and the procedures to follow. Familiarizing yourself with these details not only gives you an advantage in court but also ensures you comply with all legal requirements.

Key Aspects of State-Specific Custody Regulations

While general custody principles apply across the U.S., states differ in several key areas. Here are some aspects where variations are common:

1. Standards for Determining Custody

Most states use the "best interests of the child" standard, but how it's interpreted may vary. For instance:

- **California:** Prioritizes the child's health, safety, and welfare while also considering the benefit of frequent contact with both parents.
- **Texas:** Uses a broader range of factors, including the parents' cooperation and the child's wishes if they are 12 or older.

Some states emphasize maintaining continuity in the child's life, particularly regarding schooling, friendships, and existing routines.

2. Custody Terminology

States may use different terms for the same concepts. For example:

- In Michigan, "physical custody" refers to where the child lives, while "legal custody" covers decision-making.
- In Washington, terms like "residential schedule" replace "physical custody."

Some states avoid terms like "custodial parent" altogether and use "parenting arrangements."

3. Preference for Joint Custody

Many states, like Florida and Arizona, have laws encouraging joint custody arrangements unless there's a clear reason why it's not in the child's best interest. Courts in these states often favor shared parenting to ensure both parents remain actively involved.

4. Child's Preference

States differ on whether and how the child's preference is considered.

- **Georgia:** Allows children aged 14 or older to choose their custodial parent unless the choice is deemed harmful.
- **New York:** Considers the child's opinion but does not set a specific age threshold.

5. Relocation Laws

States have distinct rules about relocating with a child.

- **Illinois:** Requires the custodial parent to seek court approval for moves beyond 25 miles.
- **Nevada:** Has strict relocation laws, requiring clear evidence that the move benefits the child.

Steps to Understand Your State's Custody Laws

1. Research Your State's Family Code

- Take the time to research your state's family law statutes online, as understanding these laws is crucial when navigating a custody case. Most states provide this information online.
- Pay close attention to sections discussing custody, parenting plans, and visitation rights.

2. Review Relevant Case Law

In some states, precedent from past custody cases can influence decisions. Reading summaries of similar cases can provide insight into how courts typically rule.

3. Consult a Family Law Attorney

A lawyer with experience in your state can help interpret the law and explain how it applies to your specific case.

4. Attend Parenting Classes if Required

States like Tennessee mandate parenting classes for divorcing parents involved in custody disputes. Completing these classes shows the court your commitment to co-parenting effectively.

Common State-Specific Custody Processes

1. Mediation Requirements

Some states, like California and New York, require parents to attend mediation sessions before proceeding to court. This process encourages parents to resolve disputes amicably.

2. Parenting Plan Submission

States like Oregon and Minnesota place a strong emphasis on creating detailed parenting plans that clearly outline custody arrangements, visitation schedules, and decision-making responsibilities. These plans are not just formalities but helps to minimize disputes between parents and establish clear expectations.

3. Custody Evaluations

Courts in states such as Florida may order a custody evaluation conducted by a psychologist or social worker. These evaluations assess each parent's ability to meet the child's needs.

Challenges Fathers Face in State-Specific Regulations

As a father, you might encounter hurdles due to outdated stereotypes or inconsistent application of laws. However, many states are working toward gender-neutral custody standards.

Showing your dedication as an engaged parent can help counteract any biases.

Tips for Fathers Navigating State-Specific Custody Laws

1. Stay Informed

Laws can change, so regularly review updates to your state's custody regulations.

2. Build a Strong Case

Collect evidence of your involvement in your child's life, such as school records, doctor visits, and extracurricular activities.

3. Cooperate with the Other Parent

Courts in most states prioritize cooperative co-parenting over conflict when determining custody arrangements, as they recognize that children thrive in environments where their parents work together harmoniously.

4. Follow Court Orders

Even if you disagree, adhering to interim orders demonstrates your respect for the legal process.

Strategic Suggestions

- Learn the specific laws in your state to tailor your custody strategy effectively. Familiarity with these regulations shows you are serious about your parental responsibilities.
- Prepare a detailed parenting plan that aligns with your state's requirements. Highlight your willingness to work collaboratively while emphasizing the benefits for your child.
- Engage with local support groups or organizations that advocate for fathers' rights. They can provide guidance specific to your state.

State-specific custody regulations may seem complex, but with careful research and preparation, you can use this knowledge to strengthen your position in court. Understanding your state's unique laws empowers you to advocate effectively for your child and yourself.

Chapter 2: Assessing Your Situation

Assessing your situation involves evaluating your current parenting role, resources, and the factors that influence your child's well-being. This step is crucial for understanding your strengths and addressing any challenges in a custody case. A clear perspective allows you to plan effectively and demonstrate your ability to provide a stable environment.

Evaluating Your Parental Role and Contributions

Winning custody begins with understanding the value you bring to your child's life. As a father, you play a crucial role in shaping your child's emotional, mental, and physical well-being. To present your case effectively, it's essential to evaluate your parental role and contributions honestly and thoroughly.

Understanding Your Role as a Father

Your involvement as a father goes beyond financial support. It includes emotional connection, day-to-day caregiving, and being a positive influence in your child's development. Start by reflecting on how you participate in your child's life, including:

1. Daily Routines

- Do you help with morning routines, school drop-offs, or bedtime rituals?

- Are you actively involved in your child's homework, meals, or extracurricular activities?

2. Emotional Support

- Are you available when your child needs comfort or advice?
- Do you celebrate their achievements and help them navigate challenges?

3. Special Moments

- Have you created memorable experiences, such as outings, birthdays, or vacations?
- Do you show interest in your child's hobbies and talents?

Evaluating these aspects highlights how you contribute to your child's stability and happiness.

Tracking Your Contributions

Once you've identified your role, it's important to document your contributions. Courts appreciate factual evidence over emotional claims, so detailed records can significantly strengthen your case.

1. Financial Contributions

- Keep proof of expenses, including child support payments, healthcare costs, school fees, and clothing purchases.
- If you've gone above and beyond with gifts or extracurricular fees, document those as well.

2. Time Spent Together

- Maintain a calendar of time spent with your child, such as weekends, holidays, or school events.
- Note specific activities, like attending parent-teacher meetings, coaching a sports team, or helping with projects.

3. Communication Records

- Save texts, emails, or call logs showing your involvement in your child's life.

- Examples could include planning schedules, checking on their well-being, or collaborating with the other parent.
- Being organized with evidence not only reflects your dedication but also makes your case more compelling.

Identifying Areas for Improvement

No parent is perfect, and recognizing where you can grow is part of being a responsible father. Courts value parents who demonstrate a willingness to improve for their child's benefit.

1. Time Commitment

- If your work or personal life has limited your availability, consider ways to adjust. Can you rearrange your schedule to spend more time with your child?

2. Co-Parenting Skills

Are you cooperative with the other parent? Courts favor parents who can communicate effectively and prioritize the child over conflict.

3. Home Environment

- Ensure your home is safe, clean, and child-friendly. Provide a dedicated space for your child to sleep, study, and play.

Common Mistakes to Avoid

1. Underestimating Your Role

- Many fathers overlook their contributions, assuming they're less significant than the mother's. Recognize the unique value you bring as a father.

2. Being Reactive Instead of Proactive

- Don't wait for issues to arise before taking action. Being prepared shows you're consistently involved and dependable.

3. Lack of Documentation

- Without evidence, it's hard to prove your involvement. Regularly update your records to ensure nothing is overlooked.

Practical Steps to Evaluate Your Role

- Start a parenting journal where you record daily or weekly activities with your child. This simple habit can highlight your efforts and provide useful evidence.
- Engage in your child's interests, which may be a sport, hobby, or game. Showing enthusiasm strengthens your bond and demonstrates active involvement.
- Schedule one-on-one time with your child regularly. Quality time matters as much as quantity and leaves a lasting impact on their development.

Strategic Suggestions

- Be consistent in your involvement. Courts value reliability, so ensure your efforts aren't sporadic.
- Focus on quality parenting. It's not just about spending time; it's about how you use that time to support, teach, and connect with your child.

- Stay positive when discussing your role. Avoid blaming the other parent or highlighting their shortcomings—focus on your strengths and contributions instead.

Evaluating your parental role and contributions gives you a clearer picture of your impact on your child's life. It also prepares you to confidently present your case in court, demonstrating that you're an engaged, loving father who prioritizes their child's best interests.

Recognizing Potential Custody Challenges

As a father preparing for a custody battle, it's important to recognize the potential challenges you may face. Custody disputes can be complex and emotionally charged, and understanding the obstacles ahead allows you to better plan and respond. Knowing these challenges can help you avoid common pitfalls, prepare strong arguments, and advocate effectively for your role as a father.

Challenges in Gaining Custody as a Father

While laws have become more gender-neutral over time, fathers still sometimes face biases in custody cases. It's essential to recognize the hurdles that may arise and be ready to address them.

1. Gender Bias

Historically, courts have favored mothers in custody decisions, particularly in cases of young children. Although many courts now prioritize the child's best interests, this bias can still exist, and it may be something you need to overcome. Courts may assume that mothers are more suited for the primary caregiving role, even if you've been equally involved in your child's life.

What You Can Do: Focus on showing that you can provide the same level of care and stability that a mother can. Document your active involvement and emphasize your ability to co-parent effectively.

2. Perceptions of Fathers as Secondary Caregivers

There is often a perception that fathers are secondary caregivers, typically taking on less responsibility in daily parenting tasks. While this has changed over the years, some people still hold these outdated views.

What You Can Do: Make sure to highlight your day-to-day contributions, including providing emotional support, helping with homework, and participating in medical and school appointments. The more you can prove your hands-on role, the stronger your position will be.

3. The Other Parent's Influence

The other parent may attempt to undermine your relationship with your child or present you in a negative light. This could include accusations about your parenting, behavior, or even your relationship with your child. In some cases, parental alienation can occur, where one parent intentionally tries to distance the child from the other parent.

What You Can Do: If this happens, keep detailed records of interactions and communication. If possible, involve a neutral third party or counselor to mediate or observe situations where conflict arises. Courts take these allegations seriously, so the more proof you have to counteract any false claims, the better.

External Factors That May Influence Custody Decisions

In addition to challenges directly related to you and your co-parent, external factors can play a significant role in the court's decision-making process. Recognizing these can help you anticipate what to expect.

1. The Child's Relationship with Each Parent

If the child has a stronger attachment or a deeper bond with one parent, it may influence the court's decision. This is especially true if the child expresses a preference for one parent over the other, though this typically happens when the child is old enough to make their wishes known.

What You Can Do: Work on building a strong emotional connection with your child, engaging in activities that foster trust and understanding. If possible, document positive interactions that show your active role in the child's life.

2. Stability of Each Parent's Home

Courts want to ensure that children grow up in a stable, safe environment. If your living situation is less stable—such as if you've recently moved or have an unstable income—it could be viewed as a potential concern.

What You Can Do: Ensure that your home is child-friendly and secure. If there are issues with stability, work towards resolving them, such as securing a more permanent living arrangement or addressing financial concerns.

3. Work Schedule and Availability

The court will assess whether you can provide the time and attention your child needs. If your work schedule conflicts with your ability to care for your child, this may be seen as a challenge in gaining custody.

What You Can Do: If you have an inflexible work schedule, consider making adjustments or offering a plan for shared custody that prioritizes the child's needs. If you're able to arrange time off or flexible hours to be more available, demonstrate this to the court.

4. Legal and Procedural Hurdles

Beyond personal and external challenges, there are legal and procedural hurdles that can make custody cases difficult for fathers. Understanding these will help you prepare for potential roadblocks.

5. Legal Costs and Representation

Custody battles are costly, especially if you need legal representation. Legal fees, filing costs, and expert evaluations can add up quickly.

What You Can Do: Look into resources that might help reduce costs, such as legal aid or pro bono services. Consider working with a lawyer who specializes in fathers' rights or custody disputes to guide you through the process.

6. Complexity of Custody Agreements

Custody arrangements can be intricate and involve multiple steps, including temporary custody orders, mediation, and possibly a custody evaluation. If you and your co-parent can't agree, the process may drag on longer than expected.

What You Can Do: Be prepared for the process to take time. Stay organized, keep track of deadlines, and remain patient. If you can, try to negotiate an agreement with your co-parent rather than going to trial, as this can save both time and emotional energy.

7. Emotional and Personal Struggles

Custody battles are emotionally draining. As a father, it can be overwhelming to navigate the process while dealing with the emotions of being separated from your child. The stress can sometimes cloud your judgment or make you feel like giving up.

8. Emotional Strain on You and Your Child

Prolonged custody battles can take an emotional toll on both you and your child. Children often feel torn between parents and may struggle with stress, anxiety, or confusion.

What You Can Do: Prioritize your child's emotional well-being. Be patient, calm, and understanding. If possible, seek family counseling or therapy to help both you and your child process the situation together.

9. Managing Stress

The custody process can bring out feelings of frustration, anger, or hopelessness. These emotions can affect your ability to make sound decisions.

What You Can Do: Find healthy outlets for stress, such as exercise, meditation, or talking to a trusted friend or therapist. Keep a clear head so you can make decisions that are in the best interest of your child.

Strategic Suggestions

- **Prepare for Bias:** Understand that some bias may still exist, so be proactive in presenting yourself as an involved and capable parent.

- **Maintain a Stable Environment:** Work towards creating a stable, safe, and nurturing home environment for your child, as this is a key factor in custody decisions.

- **Document Everything:** Keep detailed records of your interactions with your child and co-parent, especially if you anticipate challenges related to custody.

- **Stay Calm and Focused:** The emotional and personal challenges are real, but keeping a clear head and staying focused on your child's best interests will be your best asset.

Recognizing potential custody challenges gives you the tools to address them head-on. Prepare for these obstacles to be in a better position to advocate for yourself and ensure that your child's needs are prioritized.

Identifying the Child's Best Interests

When it comes to custody battles, the most important factor courts consider is the child's best interests. This principle guides every decision, from custody arrangements to visitation schedules. As a father, understanding what constitutes your child's best interests and how to advocate for them is essential.

The Core Principles of the Best Interests Standard

The "best interests" standard is a broad guideline that courts use to make decisions about custody and parenting time. While it can vary slightly from state to state, there are common principles that courts focus on when determining what is best for the child:

1. The Child's Safety and Well-Being

Above all, the court wants to ensure that the child is in a safe environment. This includes both physical safety (such as protection from abuse, neglect, or exposure to dangerous situations) and emotional safety (ensuring the child's mental health and stability are prioritized).

What You Can Do: Show that your home is a safe and nurturing environment. If there have been any past issues, address them directly and explain how you've made improvements for your child's well-being.

2. The Child's Relationship with Each Parent

Courts often look at the existing relationship between the child and each parent. A strong, positive relationship with both parents is seen as a key factor in the child's development.

What You Can Do: Highlight your active involvement in your child's life. Show how you maintain an open, loving relationship with them and provide for their emotional and physical needs.

3. The Child's Adjustment to Home, School, and Community

The stability of your child's current living situation plays a significant role in custody decisions. Courts are more likely to favor maintaining a familiar environment, especially if the child is well-adjusted at school, in extracurricular activities, and in their community.

What You Can Do: Demonstrate your child's involvement in the community and how your custody proposal will minimize disruption to their routine. If possible, show how you can provide consistency in their daily life.

4. The Child's Physical and Emotional Needs

The court looks at the child's specific needs, which can include everything from medical care to emotional support. For example, if your child has special needs or a medical condition, the court will consider which parent is better equipped to provide for those needs.

What You Can Do: Document any special needs your child has and show how you're able to meet those needs. Provide evidence of doctor's visits or educational support.

5. The Ability of Each Parent to Co-Parent

Courts highly value parents who can cooperate and communicate effectively in the child's best interest. A parent who is willing to work with the other parent for the child's benefit is likely to receive a more favorable custody arrangement.

What You Can Do: Prove your willingmess to work with your ex and make compromises. If you've previously had successful co-parenting experiences, highlight them.

6. The Child's Preference (When Appropriate)

As children grow older, their opinion may be taken into account. The weight given to the child's preference depends on their age, maturity, and the circumstances surrounding the case. While a child's preference may not be the deciding factor, it can certainly influence the court's decision.

What You Can Do: If your child is old enough, be sure to maintain a positive relationship so they feel comfortable expressing their preferences. Avoid pressuring your child into choosing sides, as the court values the child's opinion when it's freely given.

How to Advocate for Your Child's Best Interests

1. Build a Case Around Stability

Courts want to know that the child will have a stable environment. Stability is about more than just a steady home—it includes emotional stability, maintaining consistent routines, and having strong support systems in place.

What You Can Do: Show how your parenting plan provides for stability. This might include staying in the same home, having consistent school arrangements, and maintaining a close relationship with family and friends. If you're offering shared custody, be clear about how both parents will support the child's routines.

2. Demonstrate Your Willingness to Co-Parent

The court will evaluate how well you can work with the other parent to make joint decisions about your child's life. Courts tend to favor parents who are cooperative.

What You Can Do: Communicate with the other parent in a calm, respectful manner. Avoid negative comments about them in front of the child or in court. Show that you can compromise when needed.

3. Provide Evidence of Your Parenting Involvement

Courts appreciate fathers who are active and involved in their child's life. To support your claim of being an engaged parent, you need to provide evidence. This could be in the form of:

- Medical records showing your involvement in doctor's visits.
- School records showing you attend parent-teacher conferences or help with homework.
- Photos or logs of time spent with the child on weekends, vacations, or special events.

What You Can Do: Organize a portfolio of evidence that reflects your role in the child's life. The more thorough and consistent your documentation, the stronger your case will be.

4. Focus on the Child's Needs Over Your Own

It's easy to get caught up in your personal desires during a custody battle, but the court is primarily concerned with what is best for the child. Prioritize the child's emotional and physical needs, and avoid using the child as a pawn to hurt the other parent.

What You Can Do: When making decisions, always focus on your child's well-being. If necessary, consult with professionals like child psychologists to get a better understanding of your child's needs.

Strategic Suggestions

- **Create a Parenting Plan:** Courts often favor parents who propose a clear and detailed parenting plan. This plan should focus on the child's needs and demonstrate how both parents will share responsibilities.
- **Show Emotional Availability:** Ensure that your child knows you are always there for them emotionally. Be open to listening and providing support as they process any changes.
- **Maintain Consistency:** Try to keep routines consistent across both homes,

which can help the child feel more secure and stable during transitions.

Focus on your child's best interests to not only improve your chances of securing a favorable custody arrangement, but you also demonstrate your commitment to being a responsible, loving father. The more you can show that you are prioritizing your child's well-being, the more likely the court is to support your custody request.

Chapter 3: Preparing Essential Documentation

Preparing essential documentation involves gathering records that support your case and demonstrate your role as a responsible parent. This process is vital for presenting evidence that highlights your ability to meet your child's needs. Organized, thorough documentation can strengthen your position and ensure the court has a clear picture of your efforts.

Collecting Proof of Parenting Involvement

When preparing for a custody battle, one of the most important things you can do is collect solid documentation of your involvement as a parent. The court wants to see that you're not just a passive figure in your child's life but an active, consistent presence who contributes to their well-being in every way possible. This documentation can be a game-changer in demonstrating that you are a capable and involved father, just as much as your co-parent.

Why Proof of Parenting Involvement Is Crucial

The court uses proof of parenting involvement to assess the level of your commitment to your child. Courts are not looking for fathers who only appear during special occasions or when it's convenient. Instead, they want to know that you're involved in your child's day-to-day life, such as if you take them to school, attend doctor's appointments, or simply spend quality time together.

1. Shows Consistency

A key factor in custody decisions is whether a parent has consistently been present for their child. Courts prefer parents who have been consistently involved, as this suggests stability for the child.

What You Can Do: Collect evidence that shows you've been actively participating in your child's life over a long period of time.

2. Demonstrates Your Capability

Courts are not only looking for involvement but also your capability to care for your child's physical, emotional, and psychological needs. Document your active role to prove that you are more than capable of providing for your child.

What You Can Do: Keep a record of tasks you've performed that show your ability to meet your child's needs, such as managing doctor's appointments, grocery shopping, or even making decisions about their schooling.

3. Helps Counter Negative Claims

If your co-parent tries to claim that you aren't involved or are less competent as a parent, having proof of your involvement can refute those claims.

What You Can Do: Keep a log or calendar of parenting tasks and responsibilities. If there are any instances where your involvement has been questioned, you'll have the documentation to prove otherwise.

Types of Proof to Collect

Now that you understand why it's important, let's explore the different types of proof you can collect to demonstrate your involvement in your child's life.

1. Day-to-Day Parenting Tasks

These include the practical aspects of day-to-day care, like feeding, bathing, and helping with homework. These activities show that you're actively involved in your child's life in a way that goes beyond just being a presence.

What You Can Do: Keep a detailed log of tasks that you perform regularly. This can include everything from helping with school projects to attending parent-teacher meetings. If you take your child to therapy or extracurricular activities, include these in your log as well.

2. Medical and School Involvement

Courts will want to see that you are actively involved in your child's healthcare and education. Attending doctor's appointments, dentist visits, and parent-teacher conferences shows that you're not leaving these important responsibilities solely to your co-parent.

What You Can Do: Keep records of medical and school-related activities. This can include appointment cards, notes from teachers or doctors, and any communication between you and school staff. If you have signed any important medical consent forms, be sure to have copies of these too.

3. Written Communication

If you and your co-parent communicate regularly about your child, this can be an important piece of evidence. Courts appreciate evidence that you're co-parenting effectively and that you're both on the same page when it comes to decisions about your child's welfare.

What You Can Do: Keep copies of emails, text messages, or letters that show you've been actively communicating with your co-parent about your child's needs. If you've made decisions together, such as choosing a school or setting up medical appointments, this documentation is crucial.

4. Photos and Videos

Pictures and videos are powerful tools for showing your involvement. They provide tangible, visual proof of your relationship with your child and the time you spend together.

What You Can Do: Take photos or videos during key moments in your child's life, such as birthdays, holidays, or school events. These snapshots can show the bond you share with your child and prove emotionally investment.

How to Organize Your Documentation

Courts can be overwhelmed with documents, so you need to keep everything organized and easy to navigate.

1. Create a Parenting Journal

One of the most efficient ways to document your parenting involvement is by keeping a detailed parenting journal. This can include everything from daily tasks to major milestones.

What You Can Do: Start a journal or log, noting every instance in which you've been actively involved with your child. This can include small daily tasks like getting them ready for school or attending a meeting with their teacher.

2. Create Digital Copies

As much as possible, digitize your documents, especially important forms like medical records, school notes, or emails. Digital records are easier to organize, search, and share.

What You Can Do: Scan important documents and organize them in a folder on your computer or cloud storage. Label them clearly so that you can easily find what you need.

3. Organize by Categories

Sorting your proof into categories (e.g., school involvement, medical care, daily care) will make it easier for both you and the court to understand your contributions. When you present your evidence, break it down into clear sections to avoid overwhelming the court with too much information at once.

What You Can Do: Create a folder for each category: medical, educational, or personal care. For each folder, include all relevant documents, such as emails, receipts, appointment records, and photos.

4. Consult with Your Lawyer

Your lawyer will be able to guide you on the best way to organize and present your documentation. They can also tell you if there are any additional pieces of evidence that could strengthen your case.

What You Can Do: Work closely with your attorney to make sure your evidence is presented in the best possible way. They may also suggest other types of documentation that can support your claim of being an active, involved father.

Strategic Suggestions

- **Stay Consistent:** Regular documentation of your parenting involvement is critical. Even if it seems

small at the moment, the consistency of your effort will paint a powerful picture of your commitment over time.
- **Highlight Key Moments:** Focus on the moments that truly show your engagement, like doctor's appointments, school events, and personal milestones.
- **Keep It Organized:** Ensure all your proof is well-organized and easy to navigate. Clear and concise records are much more persuasive than a mountain of scattered documents.

Gathering and presenting proof of your parenting involvement can be the difference between gaining custody or losing your case. Keep thorough records and demonstrate your consistent, active role in your child's life to show the court that you are more than capable of providing the stable and loving environment your child deserves.

Organizing Financial and Employment Records

When it comes to child custody, your financial situation and job stability play a significant role in the court's decision. The court needs to ensure that both parents can provide a stable and secure environment for the child. For fathers, presenting clear, organized financial and employment records is essential to demonstrate that you are capable of supporting your child and fulfilling your parental responsibilities.

Why Financial and Employment Records Matter

Your financial and employment records provide the court with insight into your ability to support your child both now and in the future. A stable job and adequate income indicate that you are in a position to provide for your child's needs, including food, clothing, housing, education, and healthcare.

1. Proving Financial Stability

Courts prefer to see that the parent awarded custody can provide for the child without relying on others. This includes being able to meet the child's everyday needs and any potential additional expenses.

What You Can Do: Gather evidence of your income and expenses. This will help demonstrate that you have the financial capacity to care for your child.

2. Child Support Considerations

In most cases, the court will also evaluate your financial ability to contribute to child support if you are seeking joint custody or visitation rights. Having organized financial documents will allow you to show the court that you are committed to providing for your child's financial needs, regardless of the custody arrangement.

What You Can Do: Be transparent about your financial obligations and your ability to meet them. If you are already paying child support or alimony, make sure you have records of these payments to demonstrate your responsibility.

3. Job Stability and Employment History

A steady job and reliable income are important factors when determining your ability to care for your child. Courts look at employment history to ensure that you can provide long-term stability. This is especially crucial if your child is young and will need long-term financial support.

What You Can Do: Keep detailed records of your employment, including contracts, pay stubs, and any letters from your employer confirming your job stability. If you have multiple sources of income or a business, provide documentation of these as well.

Types of Financial and Employment Documents to Collect

To make sure your financial situation is clear and well-documented, here are some key records you should gather:

1. Pay Stubs and Tax Returns

Pay stubs are an excellent way to prove your monthly income. Tax returns offer a full picture of your financial history, including any deductions, dependents, or other information the court may need to know.

What You Can Do: Keep copies of your most recent pay stubs and tax returns. If you've changed jobs recently, it's important to show continuity in your income. The more recent the documents, the better, but older tax returns can help demonstrate stability over time.

2. Bank Statements

Bank statements help demonstrate your financial habits and ability to manage your finances responsibly. Regular deposits, savings, and consistency in managing your account will reflect positively in court.

What You Can Do: Collect a few months of your bank statements, particularly showing consistent deposits and withdrawals. This can help establish a pattern of responsible financial behavior.

3. Employment Contracts and Job History

Having a stable job is often a priority in custody cases. Courts like to see that you have a history of reliable employment, which will support your ability to provide for your child.

What You Can Do: Provide a copy of your employment contract or any written proof of your job position, salary, and length of employment. If you're self-employed or run a business, provide evidence of your business operations, such as invoices or tax filings.

4. Debt and Expense Records

While debts are not necessarily a dealbreaker, understanding your financial obligations helps the court make informed decisions. If you have significant debt, it may affect your ability to contribute to child support or other financial obligations.

What You Can Do: Include any documentation related to loans, mortgages, credit card payments, or other debts. This shows the court that you are financially aware and managing your responsibilities.

5. Proof of Child-Related Expenses

To demonstrate that you have been contributing to your child's financial needs, include any receipts or records that show you are providing for things like school supplies, clothing, medical bills, or extracurricular activities.

What You Can Do: Keep receipts for any child-related expenses. This shows that you've been taking responsibility for your child's financial needs and that you're proactive about their welfare.

How to Organize Your Financial and Employment Records

Once you've collected your financial documentation, it's crucial to organize everything in a way that's clear and easy to present. Courts can become overwhelmed by piles of paper, so your records should be neat and well-organized to ensure the process goes smoothly.

1. Create a Financial Portfolio

A financial portfolio is a collection of all your important financial documents. This portfolio should include pay stubs, bank statements, tax returns, employment contracts, and any other relevant documents. Make sure that all documents are current, properly filed, and easy to navigate.

What You Can Do: Create folders for each type of financial document to prove income, savings, or debts. Keep everything in chronological order to show an accurate financial history.

2. Digitize Important Documents

Physical documents can be cumbersome, and sometimes hard to organize. Digitizing your records helps you keep them safe and easily accessible.

What You Can Do: Scan all your important documents and save them in a secure digital folder. Use a cloud storage system to ensure you can access them from anywhere and to back up your files in case anything is lost.

3. Keep a Record of All Child-Related Expenses

Ensure you keep an ongoing record of any child-related expenses. This shows that you actively contribute to their upbringing.

What You Can Do: Keep a spreadsheet or log where you note every expense related to your child. You can even attach receipts or invoices as proof of financial support for your child.

4. Work with a Financial Advisor or Lawyer

If your financial situation is complex, or if you are unsure how to organize everything properly, consider seeking advice from a financial advisor or a lawyer. They can help you present your financial records in the most effective way for your custody case.

What You Can Do: Schedule a meeting with your lawyer to review your financial documents. They can help you understand which documents are most important and how to present them in court.

Strategic Suggestions

- **Be Transparent:** Always be honest about your financial situation. The court will appreciate your transparency, especially if you're going through financial difficulties. Trying to hide or misrepresent your financial situation can hurt your case.
- **Document Consistently:** Regularly update your financial records, keeping track of any significant changes in income, expenses, or obligations. This

helps demonstrate that you're financially responsible and proactive.

- **Highlight Stability:** Make sure the court understands that your financial situation is stable. Demonstrating job stability, regular income, and the ability to provide for your child will strengthen your case.

Properly organizing your financial and employment records is essential in showing that you can provide a stable, supportive environment for your child. When you present clear, well-organized documentation, you demonstrate your ability to meet your child's needs and secure a favorable custody arrangement.

Gathering Communication and Co-Parenting Logs

In a child custody case, how well you communicate and co-parent with your ex is a crucial factor in the court's decision-making process. Courts wants to know if both parents are able to work together for the benefit of their child. A positive, cooperative relationship between parents is often a sign of stability for the child. On the other hand, conflicts and poor communication can raise concerns about the child's well-being. That's why gathering a thorough log of your communication and co-parenting efforts is vital in a custody battle.

Why Communication and Co-Parenting Matter

Effective communication and co-parenting demonstrate that you are putting your child's needs first. Courts look for evidence that both parents are able to cooperate, share parenting responsibilities, and make joint decisions that are in the best interests of the child. Poor communication or constant conflict between parents can raise red flags about the child's emotional and psychological well-being.

1. Proving Your Willingness to Co-Parent

Courts appreciate when both parents are willing to work together, even if they are not in a romantic relationship. If you can show that you have been cooperative with your ex in raising your child, the court is more likely to view you as a responsible, reliable parent.

What You Can Do: Keep a record of all communication between you and your ex, especially when it comes to decisions about your child. This shows that you are engaged in the co-parenting process and committed to working together.

2. Demonstrating Your Involvement

Communication and co-parenting logs also help prove that you are actively involved in your child's life. This is crucial, as being involved doesn't just mean spending time with your child—it also means making decisions, handling logistics, and staying in touch with the other parent.

What You Can Do: Document all instances when you communicated with your ex about parenting decisions, child needs, and other important matters. This not only demonstrates your involvement but also shows your commitment to making decisions in the child's best interest.

3. Countering Claims of Irresponsibility or Neglect

If your ex accuses you of not being involved or failing to communicate, having a clear record of your interactions will help you counter these claims. It provides a factual basis to show that you have been a responsible and proactive co-parent.

What You Can Do: If there are any disputes or accusations, your communication logs can serve as evidence to defend your actions. Be sure to note any important messages or exchanges that could be used as proof of your involvement.

What to Include in Your Communication and Co-Parenting Logs

To make sure your logs are thorough and useful, there are several key pieces of information you should include. The more detailed and organized you are, the more helpful this documentation will be for your case.

1. Dates and Times of Communication

Each entry should include the date and time of communication, providing a clear timeline of your interactions with your ex.

What You Can Do: For each communication, note the time and date. If there are multiple exchanges in a single day, be sure to record them separately. This shows that you are consistently involved in discussions and decisions related to your child.

2. Content of Communication

Clearly record the details of what was discussed about your child's health, school activities, parenting decisions, or anything else. Having the content of the communication logged helps demonstrate that you are actively engaged in co-parenting.

What You Can Do: For every conversation or exchange, briefly summarize the main points. Be clear about the subject matter, and avoid personal comments or irrelevant details. Focus on anything that directly affects your child's welfare.

3. Mode of Communication

Different forms of communication (text, email, phone call, in person) may carry different weight in the eyes of the court. Written communication (texts and emails) is typically more reliable because it leaves a permanent record, whereas verbal communication may be harder to prove.

What You Can Do: Make a note of how each conversation took place. For phone calls or in-person meetings, it's helpful to follow up with a brief email or text to confirm what was discussed. This can help turn verbal exchanges into documented evidence.

4. Issues Discussed and Resolutions

Courts are interested in how you and your ex handle conflicts. When you face disagreements, do you work together to find a solution, or do you escalate the situation? Document any conflicts or problems, along with the solutions you've reached.

What You Can Do: If there were any disagreements or challenges, note how they were resolved. Did you work together to find a solution? Were compromises made? This shows your ability to problem-solve and co-parent effectively.

5. Child-Related Updates and Changes

Whenever there are updates about your child—such as changes in their schedule, health, or emotional well-being—make sure to document those, especially if you're communicating these updates with your ex. This proves that you're staying involved in your child's life.

What You Can Do: Whenever something important happens with your child, like a change in their health, schooling, or behavior, document how and when you communicated this with your ex. Make sure to include your response or any action you took based on the information.

How to Keep Your Communication Logs Organized

To ensure that your communication and co-parenting logs are useful and easy to understand, organizing them properly is key. A disorganized log can be difficult to follow and may weaken your case, so keeping everything neatly filed is crucial.

1. Create a Digital Log

Digital logs are easier to maintain, organize, and share. You can use a spreadsheet, a word document, or even a dedicated co-parenting app to keep track of all your communications. The advantage of using digital tools is that you can easily search for specific entries and access your logs from anywhere.

What You Can Do: Use a program like Google Docs, Excel, or even a specialized co-parenting app to track your communication. Be sure to keep everything in chronological order, and back up your log to avoid losing any information.

2. Use a Co-Parenting App

There are several apps designed specifically to help separated or divorced parents manage communication and co-parenting tasks. These apps often have built-in features for tracking exchanges, creating parenting schedules, and keeping everything in one place.

What You Can Do: Consider using apps like OurFamilyWizard, Cozi, or TalkingParents. These apps create a record of all interactions, making it easier to manage and provide proof of your involvement in your child's life.

3. Maintain Regular Entries

Don't wait until the end of the month or year to update your logs. Instead, make it a habit to record your communication on a regular basis. The more consistently you update your log, the more reliable and thorough it will be when it's time to present it in court.

What You Can Do: Set aside time each week to update your log. Even if there hasn't been much communication, it's important to keep your records current.

4. Consult with Your Lawyer

If you're unsure what should be documented or how to organize your logs, consult with your lawyer. They can guide you on what type of communication will be most beneficial to your case and help you format your logs in a way that will be most effective in court.

What You Can Do: Work closely with your attorney to ensure your communication and co-parenting logs are accurate and organized. They can also help you determine which records are most relevant to the court's considerations.

Strategic Suggestions

- **Stay Professional:** Keep all communication respectful and focused on your child's needs. Avoid personal conflicts or emotionally charged exchanges. This shows that you are committed to co-parenting effectively, even when things are difficult.
- **Be Consistent:** Make sure your logs are updated regularly and contain all relevant details. Courts look for consistency in communication and cooperation.
- **Highlight Cooperation:** Whenever possible, show instances where you and your ex worked together or reached agreements. Demonstrating your

willingness to co-parent amicably will strengthen your case.

Gathering communication and co-parenting logs provides valuable proof that you are engaged in raising your child and committed to a healthy co-parenting relationship. When organized and presented correctly, these records can show the court that you are a responsible, involved father who is capable of making decisions in the best interests of your child.

Chapter 4: Building a Strong Case

Preparing essential documentation involves gathering records that support your case and demonstrate your role as a responsible parent. This process is vital for presenting evidence that highlights your ability to meet your child's needs. Organized, thorough documentation can strengthen your position and ensure the court has a clear picture of your efforts.

Creating a Detailed Parenting Plan

When it comes to securing custody of your child, one of the most powerful tools you can have is a well-crafted parenting plan. This plan serves as a roadmap for how you and your co-parent will raise your child, detailing everything from custody arrangements to how major decisions are made. A clear, detailed parenting plan not only provides structure for your child's life but also shows the court that you are committed to being an active, responsible parent. It signals to the judge that you are willing to cooperate with your ex and that you've thoughtfully considered what is in your child's best interests.

What a Parenting Plan Includes

A parenting plan should be as detailed as possible, addressing various aspects of your child's life and how both parents will share responsibility. The more specific you can be, the better it is for you and your child, as it helps avoid confusion or disagreements in the future.

Below are key areas that your parenting plan should cover:

1. Custody and Visitation Schedule

The plan should clearly outline which parent will have physical custody of the child and when. This includes specifying the days and times the child will be with each parent, including weekends, holidays, and vacations.

What You Can Do: Be realistic about your work schedule and availability, as well as your child's needs. For example, if your child has a school or extracurricular activities schedule, make sure it's factored in.

2. Decision-Making Responsibilities

Some decisions in a child's life require joint decision-making, while others may fall solely to one parent. The plan should clearly define which decisions both parents will make together and which decisions each parent will have the authority to make independently.

What You Can Do: Clarify who will make decisions about things like health care, education, religious upbringing, and extracurricular activities. For example, if one parent is primarily responsible for medical decisions, this should be noted in the plan.

3. Parenting Time and Exchanges

The logistics of how your child will be exchanged between homes are also an important part of your parenting plan. Be specific about where and how exchanges will happen, especially if you and your ex live far apart or have different work schedules.

What You Can Do: If possible, establish neutral, public locations for exchanges. Keep the process calm and positive for your child's sake.

4. Holidays, Special Occasions, and Vacations

The plan should outline how holidays, birthdays, and special occasions will be divided between parents. This is often an area where conflict can arise, so it's important to be clear from the beginning.

What You Can Do: Make sure holidays are divided fairly and consider rotating them each year. You could alternate major holidays like Christmas, Thanksgiving, or even your child's birthday.

5. Dispute Resolution

No parenting plan is perfect, and disagreements may arise. A good plan will include a mechanism for resolving conflicts without going back to court.

What You Can Do: Agree on a dispute resolution process that works for both parents, such as using a mediator to resolve disagreements.

6. Financial Responsibilities

The plan should include how financial responsibilities for the child will be divided.

This includes child support, health insurance, and expenses related to school, extracurricular activities, and medical needs.

What You Can Do: Be transparent about your financial situation and agree on a fair division of costs. This will help prevent conflicts later on.

Why a Detailed Parenting Plan Helps Your Case

1. Shows Commitment to Your Child

A detailed plan demonstrates to the court that you are serious about being involved in your child's life. It shows that you are thinking ahead and making decisions that will benefit your child in the long term.

What You Can Do: Avoid a vague or overly simple plan. This reflects your dedication to your child's well-being.

2. Reduces Conflicts with Your Ex

The clearer the expectations are, the fewer opportunities there will be for misunderstandings and arguments. A detailed plan sets clear boundaries for both parents and creates a stable environment for your child.

What You Can Do: Address potential problem areas in advance, like holidays or decision-making, to prevent future conflicts. A clear plan helps both parents know exactly what's expected.

3. Demonstrates Your Ability to Co-Parent

A solid parenting plan highlights your willingness and ability to work cooperatively with your ex. It shows that you are able to make joint decisions for the benefit of your child and that you are capable of maintaining a civil relationship for the sake of your child's future.

What You Can Do: Keep the language in your plan neutral and positive. Avoid using it as an opportunity to air grievances or make accusations. A collaborative tone will show the court that you can work together with your ex.

4. Helps the Court Make a Fair Decision

Judges look for stability, consistency, and fairness when making custody decisions. A parenting plan that reflects these principles will likely be seen as favorable in the eyes of the court.

What You Can Do: Be fair and flexible with your co-parent. If you're requesting a specific custody arrangement, be ready to justify why it's in your child's best interest. Consider what's realistic, and be open to negotiation.

How to Create a Parenting Plan

Creating a detailed parenting plan involves open communication with your ex, keeping the child's best interests in mind, and understanding the legal requirements in your state. Here are the steps to follow:

1. Open the Dialogue with Your Ex

It's important to approach your ex in a calm and constructive way when discussing the plan. Try to avoid conflict and focus on what's best for your child. If direct communication is difficult, consider working with a mediator.

What You Can Do: Start by discussing the most important aspects of the plan, like custody time, school schedules, and holidays. Listen to your ex's concerns and work together to find a solution that works for both of you.

2. Research State Guidelines

Every state has different laws regarding child custody and what should be included in a parenting plan. Make sure you understand the guidelines in your state and how they apply to your situation.

What You Can Do: Research online or consult with a family lawyer to make sure you're familiar with the laws in your area. You can also ask your lawyer to help draft the plan.

3. Be Flexible and Reasonable

While it's important to have a detailed plan, it's also essential to remain flexible. Life changes, and your parenting plan should be adaptable. You may need to make adjustments as your child grows or as circumstances evolve.

What You Can Do: Be open to revisiting the plan after a set period to see if it's still working for everyone involved. A flexible attitude shows that you're focused on what's best for your child.

4. Document the Plan

Once you and your ex have agreed on the details, it's essential to put the plan in writing. This provides a clear record that can be referred to if needed and can help resolve disputes in the future.

What You Can Do: Make sure both you and your ex sign the parenting plan. It's also helpful to have a lawyer review the document to ensure that it's legally sound and enforceable.

Strategic Suggestions

- **Prioritize Your Child's Needs:** Focus on what's in your child's best interest rather than your personal preferences.

This is crucial in convincing the court that you are committed to providing a stable, supportive environment.

- **Maintain a Positive Tone:** Keep the language in your parenting plan neutral and positive. A collaborative, respectful attitude will strengthen your case and make it easier to work with your ex.
- **Be Thorough but Flexible:** While your plan should be detailed, also be open to making adjustments as necessary. Flexibility demonstrates your willingness to adapt to your child's changing needs.

Creating a detailed parenting plan is one of the most important steps in securing custody. A well-thought-out plan can help reduce conflict, show your commitment as a parent, and provide a stable environment for your child. Take the time to create a clear, fair, and realistic plan that prioritizes your child's needs, and you'll be one step closer to winning your custody battle.

Understanding What Judges Look For

When going through a child custody battle, it's important to know what judges are looking for when making their decision. Judges aren't just considering the parents' wishes but, most importantly, what is best for the child. Understanding the factors that influence a judge's decision will give you a better chance of presenting a case that aligns with those priorities. As a father, it's essential to be prepared and informed on what judges value most in child custody cases.

What Judges Prioritize in Custody Cases

While every case is unique, there are several key factors that most judges will take into consideration when deciding on custody arrangements. These factors revolve around the child's best interests, which is the primary concern in any custody case.

1. The Child's Relationship with Each Parent

Judges want to see a stable and loving relationship between the child and both parents. The more involved and present you are in your child's life, the more likely you are to be awarded custody. Judges will look at your history with your child—your day-to-day involvement, emotional bond, and consistency in meeting their needs.

What You Can Do: Document your involvement in your child's life. Show up for school events, doctor's appointments, extracurricular activities, and day-to-day routines. A record of consistent involvement is key.

2. The Child's Wishes (Depending on Age and Maturity)

In some cases, the judge will take into account the child's preferences. The child's wishes will carry more weight as they get older, especially if they can express themselves clearly about where they want to live or which parent they feel most comfortable with.

What You Can Do: Foster open, honest communication with your child. However, don't try to influence their decision. Let them feel safe expressing their preferences without pressure.

3. Parental Cooperation and Ability to Co-Parent

Judges want to see that both parents can work together for the benefit of the child. If one parent is constantly undermining the other or engaging in behavior that makes co-parenting difficult, the judge may view this negatively. The ability to communicate and work out differences for the child's well-being is a strong factor in a judge's decision.

What You Can Do: Keep the focus on your child. Avoid getting into personal conflicts with your ex, especially in front of your child. A positive co-parenting relationship will make the judge more likely to award joint custody.

4. Stability and Continuity

Stability is crucial when it comes to custody decisions. Judges want to maintain as much continuity as possible for the child. A stable home environment, consistent schooling, and the ability to maintain regular routines all contribute to this factor.

What You Can Do: Show that you can provide a stable living environment. This could include your job security, stable housing, and commitment to maintaining routines that support your child's growth and development.

5. The Parents' Mental and Physical Health

A parent's mental and physical health can have a significant impact on their ability to care for their child. Judges want to ensure that both parents are capable of meeting their child's needs. Issues such as substance abuse, untreated mental health issues, or a history of domestic violence could all negatively affect a parent's custody chances.

What You Can Do: Demonstrate that you are in good physical and mental health. If you have struggled in the past with any of these issues, showing that you've sought treatment or taken steps to address them will help your case.

6. The Child's Needs

Every child has different needs depending on their age, temperament, and any special circumstances they may have. For example, younger children may need more consistent contact with both parents, while older children may be more self-sufficient. Special needs children may require additional support, which a judge will consider when making a decision.

What You Can Do: Be prepared to show how your home environment meets the specific needs of your child. For example, if your child has special needs, demonstrate your ability to provide the necessary care and support.

7. History of Abuse or Neglect

Any history of abuse or neglect is taken very seriously by judges. This includes physical, emotional, or sexual abuse, as well as neglect of the child's needs. A judge will ensure that the child is safe and protected from any harm. If there's evidence of abuse, the offending parent will likely be granted limited custody or visitation rights.

What You Can Do: Ensure that your relationship with your child is healthy and free from any form of abuse. If you have concerns about the other parent's behavior, raise these issues with your attorney and ensure that they are handled properly in court.

How to Make Your Case Stand Out

Understanding what judges prioritize is crucial, but how you present your case also matters.

Here are some steps you can take to strengthen your case:

1. Show Your Involvement

Judges will look closely at how involved you've been in your child's life. If you're an active participant in school events, healthcare, or daily routines, it will work in your favor. Be proactive in showing your involvement with your child.

What You Can Do: Keep a log of important activities, such as doctor's appointments, school meetings, and events where you've been involved. This will show the court that you are consistently engaged in your child's life.

2. Be Professional and Respectful in Court

How you present yourself in court can make a big difference in how the judge perceives you. A calm, respectful demeanor will show the court that you are a responsible and mature parent.

What You Can Do: Dress professionally for court and maintain a respectful tone when addressing the judge or your ex. Avoid displaying anger or frustration, as this can hurt your case.

3. Provide Documentation

When making your case, supporting documentation can be crucial. This can include anything from school records to medical history, along with proof of your involvement in your child's life.

What You Can Do: Gather all necessary documents, such as school reports, medical records, and any communication with your ex regarding your child. This documentation will provide concrete evidence of your involvement and commitment.

4. Hire an Experienced Attorney

Having a family law attorney who understands the intricacies of custody cases can greatly improve your chances. They can help you understand the legal framework, provide advice on how to present your case, and advocate for your rights in front of the judge.

What You Can Do: Work closely with your attorney to ensure that you are fully prepared for your custody hearings. They will be able to guide you on what to expect and how to handle potential challenges.

Strategic Suggestions

- **Stay Child-Focused:** Keep the focus on what's best for your child. The court is primarily concerned with the child's well-being, so any arguments you make should center around how your proposed custody arrangement benefits your child.
- **Maintain Emotional Control:** During custody hearings, emotions can run high. However, it's important to stay calm and composed, as this will show the judge that you are capable of making decisions that are in your child's best interests.

- **Prepare for Potential Obstacles:** Understand that there may be challenges in the custody battle. Your ex might raise issues that you didn't anticipate, so be prepared to address these calmly and with solid evidence.

In a custody case, judges are primarily focused on the child's well-being. Demonstrate your involvement in your child's life, so your ability to co-parent, and your commitment to their needs, you increase your chances of a favorable ruling. Keep in mind that each case is unique, but understanding what judges prioritize is crucial to presenting a strong case for custody.

Avoiding Common Mistakes

When fighting for custody, fathers can sometimes make errors that inadvertently harm their chances. Navigating a custody battle is a high-stakes situation, and while it's easy to become emotionally charged, avoiding mistakes can be just as crucial as making the right moves. The good news is that many of these missteps are avoidable with careful planning and self-awareness. Let's take a look at some of the most common mistakes fathers make in custody battles and how you can avoid them.

1. Being Reactive Instead of Proactive

One of the biggest mistakes that fathers make in child custody cases is failing to anticipate potential challenges and waiting until something goes wrong to react. If you only react when something negative happens, such as your ex making accusations or trying to limit your time with the child, you may miss opportunities to strengthen your case. Custody battles are stressful, and it's easy to get caught off guard, but the key to success lies in being proactive.

What You Can Do: Start early and take control of your case from the beginning. Stay organized and gather all the necessary documentation—medical records, school reports, communication with your child, and evidence of your involvement in their life. If you anticipate challenges, discuss them with your attorney so you can address them early on. Being proactive allows you to handle situations before they escalate and shows the court you are taking your role as a parent seriously.

2. Failing to Communicate Effectively with Your Ex

In many cases, communication with your ex will be a critical component of the custody battle. However, a lack of communication or hostile interactions can hurt your chances. Courts generally favor parents who can cooperate and communicate respectfully for the child's well-being. If your ex feels that you are uncooperative or if communication breaks down, this can be used against you in court.

What You Can Do: Focus on maintaining calm and constructive communication with your ex. Set clear boundaries, and always keep the child's best interests at the forefront of your conversations. Keep a record of communications to ensure there is a paper trail in case the court needs evidence of your attempts at cooperation. If necessary, you can use mediation or a co-parenting counselor to help facilitate communication.

3. Not Keeping Track of Parenting Time

It's easy to assume that the court will recognize how involved you are in your child's life, but unless you can prove it, your efforts may not be given the weight they deserve. Fathers often underestimate the importance of keeping track of their parenting time. Without proof, it may be difficult to demonstrate that you are consistently providing for your child's needs.

What You Can Do: Keep a detailed log of your parenting time, including dates, times, and activities you've engaged in with your child. Document anything that showcases your involvement, such as attending appointments, helping with homework, or being part of family events. This evidence can be vital in proving your commitment to your child's upbringing. Additionally, maintain a calendar that reflects your regular visitation and parenting involvement.

4. Allowing Emotions to Overrule Rational Decisions

In the heat of a custody battle, it's easy to let emotions take control, especially when you feel that your rights are being threatened. Some fathers react impulsively—fighting aggressively for custody or saying things they might regret. Unfortunately, making decisions driven by anger, frustration, or resentment can severely damage your case. Judges are looking for calm, reasonable parents who are focused on the child's best interests, not on revenge or personal animosity.

What You Can Do: Try to remain calm and composed throughout the process. If you feel overwhelmed by emotions, take a step back and reflect before responding. It's natural to feel frustrated, but keeping a level head will show the judge that you can make thoughtful, reasoned decisions for your child. Always remember that the focus is on your child's well-being, not on settling personal scores.

5. Ignoring the Importance of Your Child's Relationship with the Other Parent

While it may seem like the best way to fight for custody is to emphasize your superior parenting abilities, it's essential not to disregard the other parent's role in the child's life. Judges generally do not want to see one parent trying to alienate the child from the other parent. A parent who speaks negatively about the other parent, attempts to limit visitation, or prevents the child from having a relationship with the other parent can seriously damage their own case.

What You Can Do: Be supportive of your child's relationship with their other parent, even if the relationship with your ex is strained. Encouraging your child to maintain a healthy bond with both parents shows maturity and is in line with what the court views as beneficial for the child. You can also document instances where you've supported the other parent's relationship with your child, as this can highlight your willingness to cooperate.

6. Not Seeking Professional Help When Needed

Another common mistake is failing to seek professional help when necessary. Family law is complex, and the custody process is challenging for any parent. Many fathers try to navigate the system on their own or underestimate the importance of having the right support team, which may include an experienced family lawyer, a counselor for emotional support, or even a parenting coordinator if needed.

What You Can Do: Hire an experienced family law attorney who understands your rights and can guide you through the process. Don't hesitate to seek therapy or counseling for yourself to handle the emotional stress. If needed, consider a co-parenting coach or mediator to help resolve conflicts with your ex, which can ultimately help your case. You don't have to do this alone, and having the right support can make a significant difference.

7. Disregarding the Importance of Stability

Fathers sometimes overlook the significance of providing a stable and consistent home environment. Judges are often concerned with the ability of each parent to provide stability for the child, particularly in terms of living arrangements, school consistency, and emotional support. Instability related to housing, employment, or relationship issues, can lead to a perception that you are not prepared to meet your child's needs in a steady way.

What You Can Do: Ensure that you have a stable living situation and a solid plan for your child's routine. Judges want to see that you can provide security in all aspects of their life— emotionally, financially, and physically. Demonstrating that you are stable in your job, housing, and lifestyle will reassure the court that your child will thrive in your care.

Strategic Suggestions

- **Stay Organized:** Keep track of everything. Logs, calendars, and records will be invaluable when it comes to showing your involvement in your child's life.
- **Remain Neutral with Your Ex:** Make efforts to keep things amicable with your co-parent, focusing on what's best for the child rather than on personal conflicts.

- **Avoid Drama:** Refrain from making inflammatory statements about your ex, and do not allow your emotions to cloud your judgment. The court is looking for a calm and stable environment for your child.
- **Get the Right Help**: Legal advice, counseling, and other resources can help you navigate the complexities of a custody battle.

Fathers who are prepared, level-headed, and proactive can avoid the most common mistakes that can negatively impact their custody case. Be focused on the best interests of your child and presenting yourself as a responsible, involved parent, so you can improve your chances of a favorable outcome in your custody battle.

Chapter 5: Hiring the Right Legal Support

Hiring the right legal support involves choosing an attorney with the expertise and experience to advocate effectively for your custody goals. This decision is critical, as skilled representation can make a significant difference in the outcome of your case. A knowledgeable lawyer provides guidance, protects your rights, and strengthens your position.

Choosing an Experienced Custody Lawyer

When you are facing a child custody battle, one of the most important decisions you'll make is choosing the right lawyer. Having the right legal representation can make a huge difference in the outcome of your case. You need a lawyer who not only understands the law but also knows how to navigate the often complex emotional and practical aspects of a custody dispute. So, how do you choose the right attorney for your situation? Let's break it down step by step.

Understanding What Makes a Good Custody Lawyer

Not all lawyers are the same, and not all lawyers are well-suited for child custody cases. While you may be tempted to hire someone who handles general family law matters or even a friend or relative who practices law, custody cases require specific experience and expertise.

A lawyer who specializes in family law, and more specifically child custody, will know the intricacies of your case, be familiar with the local court system, and be able to help you build a strong case.

1. Specialization Matters

A lawyer who specializes in family law has experience in dealing with the nuances of child custody laws and how they apply in your state. They will be up to date on the latest changes in family law and understand how judges typically rule in custody cases. It's important that the lawyer you choose has the experience and understanding to guide you through what can often be a long and challenging process.

2. Experience with Fathers' Rights

Not all family lawyers have experience advocating for fathers' rights in custody disputes. It's crucial to find a lawyer who is sympathetic to your position as a father and understands the challenges you may face. A lawyer with experience advocating for fathers can help you navigate any biases that might exist in the court system and ensure that your role as an involved parent is recognized.

Researching Potential Lawyers

Once you understand what type of lawyer you need, the next step is to find potential candidates. There are several ways to begin your search:

1. Referrals

One of the best ways to find a trusted lawyer is through word of mouth. Ask friends, family, or colleagues who have been through similar situations if they can recommend an attorney. Personal recommendations can often lead to finding someone who has a proven track record of success.

2. Online Resources

The internet is a valuable tool in your search for the right lawyer. Look at law firm websites to see if they specialize in family law and child custody.

Pay attention to client reviews, testimonials, and case results to gauge their effectiveness. You can also use online legal directories that list lawyers by area of expertise and location.

3. Bar Association Listings

Most states have a bar association that can provide a list of licensed lawyers in your area. These listings can help you find a lawyer who is qualified to handle your custody case. You can also check if the lawyer has any disciplinary actions on their record by searching for them in your state's bar association.

4. Evaluating a Lawyer's Experience

Once you have a list of potential lawyers, it's time to start narrowing them down based on their experience and qualifications. Consider the following factors:

5. Years of Practice

While a newer lawyer may have enthusiasm and modern legal knowledge, a lawyer with years of experience in family law and custody cases can offer a greater level of expertise. Experience counts when it comes to negotiating settlements or representing clients in court.

6. Success Rate in Custody Cases

Ask the lawyer about their track record in child custody cases, especially those involving fathers. While no lawyer can guarantee a specific outcome, they should be able to give you a general sense of their success in similar cases.

7. Familiarity with Local Judges and Courts

The best custody lawyers are often those who are familiar with the judges and courts in your area. If your lawyer knows how the local judges tend to rule in custody cases, they will have a better chance of guiding you through the process. They can also help you anticipate the court's needs and prepare for any potential roadblocks.

Questions to Ask During the Consultation

Meeting with a potential lawyer before hiring them is essential. Most family lawyers offer a free or low-cost initial consultation. This is your chance to ask questions and assess whether they are the right fit for your case. Here are some important questions to ask:

- How many child custody cases have you handled?
- Do you have experience representing fathers in custody cases?
- What is your strategy for handling cases like mine?
- How do you charge for your services (flat rate, hourly, or retainer)?
- What do you think are the chances of success in my case?
- How will you keep me informed about the progress of my case?

Your goal during this consultation is to ensure that the lawyer is knowledgeable, approachable, and has a clear strategy for how they would handle your case.

Understanding the Lawyer's Approach and Communication Style

Choosing a lawyer isn't just about their legal experience; it's also about how well you can work together. You need a lawyer who listens to you, respects your concerns, and communicates clearly. If you don't feel comfortable with the lawyer or if you feel that they aren't genuinely invested in your case, it may be time to consider someone else.

1. Compatibility

Look for a lawyer who understands your concerns and makes you feel heard. You want someone who is empathetic and patient but also confident and assertive when needed.

2. Clear Communication

A good lawyer will explain legal concepts in a way that is easy to understand. They should keep you updated on the progress of your case and be available when you have questions. Clear communication is essential for a successful working relationship.

Strategic Suggestions

- **Specialize in Family Law:** Ensure your lawyer has experience with family law, especially child custody cases involving fathers. This increases the likelihood that they understand your specific needs.
- **Do Thorough Research:** Take the time to explore online reviews, ask for referrals, and check with your state bar association. Choose a lawyer with a proven track record in custody cases.
- **Be Honest:** When meeting with potential lawyers, be completely honest about your situation. The more transparent you are, the better they can represent your case.

- **Trust Your Instincts:** You need to work closely with your lawyer, so it's important that you feel comfortable with them. If something feels off, don't hesitate to consult other lawyers until you find the right fit.

Choosing the right custody lawyer is one of the most important steps you can take to improve your chances of winning custody. Carefully select someone with experience, expertise, and the right approach, so you will have a valuable ally in your fight for your child's well-being.

Communicating Effectively with Your Attorney

Clear and effective communication with your lawyer is critical in any legal case, but it's especially important in a child custody battle. No matter if you are in the early stages of your case or are deep into negotiations, how you communicate with your attorney can significantly impact your chances of success. It's not just about what you say, but how you say it and how well you work together to achieve the best outcome for your child. Let's explore the best practices for fostering strong communication with your lawyer during your custody case.

Being Transparent and Honest

From the very beginning, it's essential to be completely transparent and honest with your attorney. This is your life, your child's future, and your rights at stake, so withholding information can be detrimental to your case.

Your lawyer needs all the facts, even the ones that might be uncomfortable or difficult to share. If there are issues from your past, like a history of substance abuse, past legal issues, or any other potentially harmful information, it's better that your attorney knows about it from you first.

Why Transparency Matters

Your lawyer can't help you effectively if they don't know the full story. Be open to allow them to plan a strategy that accounts for any challenges or potential setbacks. For example, if there are sensitive issues like a criminal record or past relationships that could come into play, your attorney can prepare to address them proactively in court.

Handling Sensitive Topics

If you feel nervous about revealing personal information, remember that lawyers are bound by confidentiality. They cannot share what you tell them without your consent. Be open about any weaknesses in your case so that your lawyer can work to address them ahead of time.

Setting Clear Expectations

One of the key aspects of effective communication is setting clear expectations from the start. Both you and your lawyer should have a mutual understanding of your goals for the custody battle. Are you seeking full custody, joint custody, or visitation rights? Are you more focused on spending as much time as possible with your child or making sure the child's emotional needs are met?

Discussing Goals and Priorities

Be clear about what is most important to you. This will help your lawyer tailor their strategy to meet those objectives. For example, if your primary goal is to ensure that your child's best interests are put first, your lawyer can help present your case with that in mind. If you want to maximize the amount of time you spend with your child, they can strategize accordingly.

Realistic Expectations

While it's essential to have clear goals, it's equally important to set realistic expectations. No lawyer can guarantee a specific outcome, and custody battles can often take unexpected turns. Understanding the potential outcomes and timeframes can help reduce stress and frustration during the process.

Responding Promptly and Responsibly

Communication is a two-way street. It's not just about what you tell your lawyer, but also how you respond to their requests for information, documents, or updates. Being responsive and responsible in your communication can help keep your case moving forward smoothly.

Provide Documents Promptly

Your lawyer may ask for important documents such as your child's school records, medical history, or proof of your involvement in your child's life. Get these to them as quickly as possible. Delaying this can slow down the process and may even harm your case if the lawyer can't present the necessary information on time.

Be Available for Discussions

Your lawyer will likely want to discuss different aspects of your case throughout the process via phone, email, or in person. It's important to remain available and responsive to their attempts to communicate with you. Responding quickly will show your commitment to the case and ensure that you don't miss important deadlines or meetings.

Keep an Open Line of Communication

Stay in regular contact with your lawyer to check on the progress of your case. Set up regular updates or meetings to discuss any developments, new evidence, or changes in strategy. Keeping the lines of communication open ensures that both you and your attorney are on the same page.

Being Organized and Prepared

One of the most effective ways to communicate with your lawyer is by being organized and prepared. When you can provide clear, concise, and well-organized information, it helps your attorney work more efficiently and focus on building the best case possible.

Keep Detailed Records

Your lawyer will need a variety of documents and evidence to support your case, such as communication logs, school records, financial documents, and parenting plans. Keep all this information in an easily accessible and organized format so that you can provide it when needed. A well-organized file can save your lawyer time and ensure that no important detail is overlooked.

Be Ready for Meetings

Before each meeting or phone call with your lawyer, make sure you're prepared. Write down the points you want to discuss, ask questions, and bring any necessary documents. Having a clear agenda for each meeting will help keep discussions focused and productive.

Stay Proactive

Instead of waiting for your lawyer to reach out to you, be proactive in keeping them informed of any new developments or concerns. If you have a change in your work schedule or if there is an issue with co-parenting that could affect your case, let your lawyer know immediately. This will give them the opportunity to address any potential issues before they become problems.

Maintaining Professionalism and Respect

Throughout your communications with your lawyer, always maintain a level of professionalism and respect. It's important to build a good working relationship, as this will make the process smoother for both you and your attorney.

Be Courteous

Even if you're frustrated or stressed, remain polite and respectful in your communications. This will help ensure that your lawyer is more likely to go the extra mile to help you with your case.

Avoid Overloading with Non-Essential Information

While it's important to be open with your lawyer, avoid overloading them with irrelevant or overly emotional information. Stick to the facts, and focus on the details that matter most to your case. This will help your lawyer concentrate on the key issues and avoid wasting time on unnecessary details.

Strategic Suggestions

Be Transparent: Share all relevant information, even if it's uncomfortable. Your lawyer needs to know everything to help you build the strongest case possible.

Set Clear Expectations: Be specific about your goals and understand what is realistic. This helps your lawyer tailor their approach to your unique situation.

Be Responsive: Answer calls and emails promptly. Stay on top of your lawyer's requests for documents or information to keep the case moving forward.

Stay Organized: Keep detailed and organized records of all relevant documents, communications, and information. This will make it easier for your lawyer to work efficiently.

Build a Respectful Relationship: Maintain a professional and courteous attitude with your lawyer. A positive relationship ensures a more productive collaboration.

Effective communication with your attorney is essential for the success of your custody case. Be transparent, set clear expectations, respond promptly, stay organized, and maintain professionalism, so you can help ensure that your lawyer is fully equipped to represent your interests and work toward securing the best possible outcome for you and your child.

Managing Legal Costs

Fighting for child custody can be an emotional and financial strain, especially if the case drags on for months or even years. Legal costs can quickly accumulate, and it's important to manage your expenses wisely to avoid unnecessary financial stress during what is already a challenging time. Let's explore how to manage legal costs effectively while still giving your case the attention it deserves.

Understanding the Costs Involved

Before diving into the ways to manage costs, it's essential to understand the various types of fees and expenses that may come with hiring an attorney for a child custody case. Legal fees can be broken down into several categories:

1. Hourly Rates

Most family law attorneys charge an hourly rate, which means you pay for the time they spend working on your case. Hourly rates can vary widely depending on the attorney's experience and the complexity of your case. Some lawyers may charge as little as $100 per hour, while others may charge $400 or more per hour.

2. Retainers

Some lawyers require a retainer, which is a lump sum of money you pay upfront to secure their services. The retainer is placed into a trust account, and the lawyer will bill against it as they work on your case. Once the retainer is exhausted, you may need to replenish it.

3. Flat Fees

In some cases, particularly for straightforward legal matters like drafting a basic parenting plan, a lawyer may charge a flat fee. This can be advantageous because it allows you to know in advance exactly how much the service will cost.

4. Additional Costs

Aside from the lawyer's fees, you may encounter other expenses. For example, you might need to pay for expert witnesses, court filing fees, mediation services, or travel expenses. These costs can add up quickly, so it's important to factor them into your budget.

Strategies for Reducing Legal Costs

While you may not be able to avoid all legal expenses, there are ways to minimize costs and avoid spending more than necessary. Here are some strategies to help you keep your legal costs under control:

1. Be Organized and Prepared

One of the simplest ways to reduce legal costs is by staying organized and prepared. The more prepared you are for meetings, hearings, and phone calls, the less time your lawyer needs to spend gathering information or answering questions. Keep all relevant documents organized and ready to present.

2. Use Your Lawyer's Time Wisely

Lawyers often charge for every minute they spend on your case, so it's important to be mindful of how you use their time. Avoid lengthy phone calls or emails unless absolutely necessary. Try to consolidate your questions and concerns into one communication, rather than contacting your lawyer multiple times a day. You might even want to prepare an agenda or list of topics for each meeting to keep things focused and on track.

3. Consider Mediation or Alternative Dispute Resolution (ADR)

If both you and the other parent are open to negotiation, mediation or ADR can be a cost-effective alternative to a lengthy court battle. Mediators help both parties find a middle ground without the need for a formal court hearing. Mediation typically costs less than going to court, and it can be less emotionally draining for all parties involved.

4. Limit Court Involvement

Going to court can be expensive, particularly if the case drags on. If possible, try to settle issues outside of court through negotiation, mediation, or collaborative law. This may involve some give-and-take, but it can help avoid costly court fees and lengthy litigation.

5. Discuss Payment Plans with Your Lawyer

Some attorneys may be willing to work out a payment plan, particularly if you are facing financial difficulties. If paying a large retainer upfront is a challenge, ask your lawyer if they can offer more flexible payment terms. Some lawyers may allow you to make monthly payments or break down their fees into smaller installments.

6. Limit Legal Complexity

If your case is relatively simple, avoid complicating things unnecessarily. For example, if both parents are in agreement on key issues like custody arrangements or visitation schedules, there's no need to escalate the situation by requesting unnecessary legal motions or additional hearings. Keeping things simple can reduce the amount of time your lawyer spends on the case.

Making the Most of Your Consultation

Initial consultations with lawyers are often free or low-cost, and they are a great opportunity to determine if a lawyer is right for you. Make the most of these meetings by being prepared and asking specific questions about costs. Here's what you should do:

1. Ask About Fees

During your consultation, ask the lawyer about their hourly rate, retainer fees, and any other costs you might incur. Make sure you understand how the lawyer charges and what you can expect to pay in total.

2. Discuss Payment Plans

If you are concerned about your ability to afford the lawyer's services, don't hesitate to ask if they offer payment plans or other options for managing costs. Some lawyers may also offer sliding scale fees depending on your financial situation.

3. Get a Cost Estimate

While every case is unique, a good lawyer should be able to give you a rough estimate of how much they expect the case to cost based on its complexity. This estimate can help you decide if this lawyer is a feasible option.

Explore Legal Aid or Pro Bono Services

If you are unable to afford the full cost of legal representation, there are several options available for reduced-cost or free legal services:

1. Legal Aid Services

Many states have nonprofit organizations that provide legal services to individuals with limited financial resources. These services are often available to those who meet specific income requirements. If you qualify, you may be able to receive help from a lawyer at little or no cost.

2. Pro Bono Services

Some attorneys offer pro bono (free) legal services for clients who cannot afford to pay. While this is more common in criminal cases, some family law attorneys may also offer pro bono assistance for custody battles.

Creating a Legal Budget

Finally, it's important to set a budget for your legal expenses. This will help you stay on track financially and avoid surprises down the road. Here are a few tips for creating a legal budget:

1. Estimate the Total Costs

Based on your lawyer's fee structure and the complexity of your case, try to estimate how much the case might cost in total. Be realistic about the time and resources it will take.

2. Set Aside a Fund

If possible, set aside a separate fund specifically for legal expenses. This will help you keep your finances organized and ensure you have enough money to cover your costs.

3. Track Expenses

Keep track of all the payments you make for legal services, including retainers, hourly fees, and any additional costs. This will help you monitor your spending and avoid going over budget.

Strategic Suggestions

- **Prepare Well:** Being organized and providing your lawyer with all necessary information upfront can reduce costs by making the process more efficient.
- **Consider Alternative Dispute Resolution:** Mediation or ADR can be a more affordable option for resolving custody issues without going to court.
- **Negotiate Payment Plans:** If necessary, discuss flexible payment options with your lawyer to spread out costs over time.

- **Explore Legal Aid and Pro Bono Services:** If you are struggling financially, consider legal aid or pro bono services to reduce your legal costs.

Managing legal costs doesn't mean you have to sacrifice the quality of representation in your custody case. Stay organized, understand how costs accumulate, and explore options to minimize expenses, so you can navigate the financial aspects of your case more effectively. The key is to approach the process with a clear plan and be proactive in managing your legal budget.

Chapter 6: Navigating Court Procedures

Navigating court procedures means understanding the steps, rules, and expectations involved in a custody case. This knowledge is essential for presenting yourself confidently and ensuring your case is heard effectively. Being well-prepared helps avoid unnecessary delays and mistakes, allowing you to focus on achieving a favorable outcome for your child.

Filing the Initial Custody Petition

When you're stepping into the custody process, the first official step is filing the custody petition. This legal document sets everything in motion, formally notifying the court and the other parent of your intention to pursue custody. Understanding the process of filing this petition and preparing yourself for what comes next is essential. Let's break down everything you need to know to get this critical step right.

What Is a Custody Petition?

A custody petition is a formal legal document you submit to the court to request custody or visitation rights. This petition outlines your relationship with your child, your desired custody arrangement, and the reasons supporting your request. The court uses this document to understand your case and schedule initial proceedings.

Filing a custody petition doesn't have to be intimidating. With preparation, you can ensure it reflects your commitment to your child and highlights your strengths as a parent.

Steps to Filing a Custody Petition

1. Determine the Correct Court:

The first step is figuring out which court has jurisdiction over your case. Typically, custody cases are handled in family or domestic relations courts in the county where the child resides. If you're unsure, contact the clerk of court for guidance.

2. Obtain the Required Forms:

Visit your local family court's website or office to get the forms for filing a custody petition. These forms vary slightly depending on your state, but they generally ask for:

- Your personal information.
- The other parent's personal information.

- Details about the child (e.g., age, school, and living arrangements).
- Your proposed custody arrangement.

3. Provide Accurate and Detailed Information:

Filling out the petition requires accuracy and attention to detail. Avoid exaggerations or incomplete responses, as errors could delay your case or hurt your credibility. Be honest about your current situation and ensure all the information you provide aligns with any supporting documents you plan to submit later.

4. State Your Custody Preferences:

Clearly outline the type of custody you're seeking (legal, physical, or both) and your proposed arrangement. If you believe shared custody is in the child's best interests, explain how you intend to collaborate with the other parent. If sole custody is your goal, provide a reasonable explanation for why you believe this is necessary.

5. File the Petition with the Court:

Once you've completed the form, submit it to the court clerk along with the filing fee. Filing fees vary by state but typically range between $100 and $400. If you cannot afford the fee, ask about a fee waiver application.

6. Serve the Petition on the Other Parent:

After filing, you must serve the other parent with a copy of the petition and a summons. This is a legal requirement to inform them of the case. You can use a professional process server, the sheriff's office, or certified mail for service. Keep the proof of service, as you'll need it for court records.

7. Wait for a Response:

The other parent will have a set period (usually 20–30 days) to respond to your petition. Their response will outline their agreement or disagreement with your proposed custody arrangement.

What to Include in Your Petition

1. Focus on the Child's Best Interests

Your petition should emphasize how your proposed arrangement benefits your child. Highlight your involvement in their life, such as helping with schoolwork, attending medical appointments, or participating in extracurricular activities.

2. Describe the Current Custody Situation

Provide details about where your child currently lives and how parenting responsibilities are divided. If there are existing issues, such as inconsistent visitation from the other parent, include these details.

3. Propose a Practical Parenting Plan

Courts appreciate when parents have a clear, workable plan. Include your ideas for visitation schedules, holiday arrangements, and how you'll handle communication between parents.

Common Challenges and How to Handle Them

1. Filing Errors

Mistakes in your paperwork can delay your case. Double-check everything before submission or seek help from a lawyer to ensure your documents are accurate.

2. Emotional Reactions from the Other Parent

Filing a custody petition often triggers strong emotions, both for you and the other parent. It's a significant step that can create tension, but staying calm and focused throughout the process is essential. Avoid confrontations, no matter how provoked you may feel, and resist the urge to react impulsively to any backlash or emotional responses from the other parent.

3. Navigating Legal Jargon

Legal forms can feel overwhelming. Many family courts offer resources, such as legal aid or self-help guides, to assist with completing forms. Don't hesitate to use these services.

How Courts Handle Custody Petitions

Once your petition is filed, the court will schedule a hearing to review the case. At this hearing, both parents will present their arguments, and the court will evaluate evidence to determine the child's best interests. Filing your petition correctly is critical because it sets the tone for the case and shapes the court's initial perception of you as a parent.

Strategic Suggestions

- **Gather Supporting Documents Early:** Collect evidence such as school records, medical reports, and proof of involvement in your child's life before filing.
- **Remain Respectful:** Avoid making negative statements about the other parent in your petition. Courts value

parents who prioritize the child's well-being over personal conflicts.

- **Seek Professional Help if Needed:** If you feel uncertain about the process, consult a custody lawyer or legal aid service to ensure your petition is filed properly.
- **Follow Deadlines Strictly:** Missing a filing deadline can harm your case. Stay organized and submit all forms on time.

Filing the initial custody petition is the first step toward securing your parental rights. Approach it with careful preparation and a clear focus on your child's needs. This will help demonstrate your dedication and set you up for success in the custody process.

Preparing for Custody Hearings

After filing your custody petition, the next critical step is preparing thoroughly for the custody hearings. These hearings are where you present your case to the court, demonstrating why your proposed custody arrangement serves your child's best interests. These hearings are your opportunity to show the court why your proposed arrangement is in the best interests of your child. Proper preparation can make a significant difference in how your case is presented and perceived.

What Happens During Custody Hearings?

Custody hearings allow the court to assess your situation, consider evidence, and hear from both parents. They're not just about legal arguments; they also help judges determine what's best for the child.

There are typically two types of custody hearings:

1. Temporary Custody Hearing

Focuses on short-term arrangements until the final decision.

2. Final Custody Hearing

The court makes a permanent decision on custody based on all evidence and testimonies.

Steps to Prepare for Custody Hearings

1. Understand the Custody Standards in Your State

Every state has its own guidelines and factors for deciding custody cases. Research these standards to understand what the court considers important. For instance, most courts focus on the child's best interests, which include stability, the child's relationship with each parent, and each parent's ability to meet the child's needs.

2. Organize Your Documentation

Gather all documents that support your case. These might include:

- Proof of your involvement in your child's life (e.g., school records, medical appointments, extracurricular activities).
- Financial records showing your ability to provide for the child.
- Communication logs with the other parent regarding co-parenting.
- Photos or videos highlighting your relationship with your child.

Having these documents well-organized in a binder or folder will help you present your case confidently.

3. Prepare Your Testimony

You'll likely have to speak in court about your parenting role. Prepare to answer questions such as:

- What is your relationship with your child like?
- How do you handle discipline and daily routines?
- What is your proposed custody arrangement, and why is it best for the child?

Practice your testimony with a trusted friend or your lawyer to ensure clarity and confidence.

4. Anticipate Challenges from the Other Parent:

The other parent may present arguments against your case. Think about potential criticisms or disputes they might bring up and prepare responses. For example:

- If they claim you're unavailable, show a schedule of your parenting involvement.
- If they question your financial stability, provide evidence of your income and budgeting for your child's needs.

5. Dress and Behave Appropriately in Court:

Your appearance and behavior send a strong message to the judge. Wear professional attire, arrive on time, and show respect to everyone in the courtroom. Avoid interruptions or emotional outbursts.

6. Work with Your Lawyer:

If you have legal representation, meet with your lawyer to review your case. They can help refine your testimony, suggest additional evidence, and guide you on courtroom etiquette.

Key Evidence to Present During Hearings

1. Parenting Records:

Show your involvement in your child's life through:

- School attendance records.
- Medical appointment logs.

- Notes from teachers or caregivers highlighting your role.

2. Financial Stability:

Providing pay stubs, tax returns, and proof of consistent child support payments (if applicable) is crucial to demonstrating your financial responsibility during a custody case. These documents show the court that you are not only capable of supporting your child but also committed to doing so consistently.

3. Communication with the Other Parent:

Logs of emails, texts, or calls can show your efforts to co-parent effectively. If there's conflict, keep the tone respectful and focused on the child's needs.

4. Witness Testimonies:

Family members, teachers, or caregivers who have observed your relationship with your child can provide valuable insight. Work with your lawyer to ensure they're prepared to testify.

Common Mistakes to Avoid

1. Overloading the Court with Irrelevant Information:

Focus on quality over quantity. Present only evidence that directly supports your case and demonstrates your commitment as a parent.

2. Speaking Negatively About the Other Parent:

Judges frown on attempts to badmouth the other parent unless it's directly relevant to the child's safety. Stay professional and focus on your strengths.

3. Ignoring Court Deadlines or Requirements:

Failing to submit documents on time or missing required obligations, such as parenting classes, can significantly harm your custody case. Courts expect parents to demonstrate responsibility and commitment throughout the process, and missing deadlines or mandatory tasks may suggest a lack of seriousness about your parental role.

What Judges Look for During Hearings

Judges consider several factors during custody hearings, including:

- Each parent's relationship with the child.
- The stability and safety of each parent's home.
- Willingness to co-parent and encourage a relationship with the other parent.
- The child's needs, including education, health, and emotional well-being.
- Being prepared and showing that you prioritize your child's best interests can leave a positive impression on the court.

Strategic Suggestions

- **Practice Clear Communication:** Speak calmly and stick to the facts. Avoid overloading your testimony with unnecessary details.

- **Keep a Positive Attitude:** Show the court that you're focused on solutions and the child's well-being.
- **Stay Organized:** Use a checklist to ensure you've gathered all necessary documents and evidence before the hearing.
- **Be Flexible:** Show a willingness to cooperate with the other parent if it benefits the child.

Preparing for custody hearings requires time, effort, and a focus on your child's needs. Stay organized, practice your testimony, and present evidence effectively to approach the court with confidence and demonstrate your dedication as a father.

Presenting Evidence and Witnesses

Presenting evidence and witnesses during a custody case can be one of the most impactful parts of the process. This is your chance to demonstrate your role as a capable and loving parent. Success here depends on preparation, clarity, and choosing evidence and witnesses that align with your child's best interests. Let's break down what you need to know to effectively make your case.

Why Evidence and Witnesses Matter

In custody battles, courts rely heavily on concrete evidence and credible witnesses to understand the family dynamic. Evidence provides factual support for your claims, while witnesses offer additional perspectives on your parenting and relationship with your child. Together, they paint a complete picture of your ability to meet your child's needs.

Steps to Present Evidence Effectively

1. Identify Relevant Evidence

Not all evidence is created equal. Focus on items that directly support your case and demonstrate your involvement in your child's life. Examples include:

- **Parenting Records:** Calendars or logs showing how often you've cared for your child.
- **Financial Records:** Proof of your ability to provide for the child, such as pay stubs, receipts for school supplies, and medical bills.
- **Photos or Videos:** Visual proof of your relationship, like pictures from birthdays, school events, or family outings.
- **Communication Logs:** Emails or texts that show your attempts to co-parent or arrange visitation schedules.

- **School and Medical Records:** Reports that demonstrate your involvement in your child's education and healthcare.

2. Organize and Label Your Evidence

Courts appreciate organization. Group your evidence by category and label it clearly. For example, you might divide it into sections like "Parenting Involvement," "Financial Stability," and "Communication."

3. Provide Copies to the Court and Other Parent

Most courts require you to submit copies of your evidence to both the court and the other parent (or their lawyer) in advance. Check the deadlines in your jurisdiction and ensure everything is submitted on time.

4. Be Ready to Explain Your Evidence:

During the hearing, the court may ask questions about your evidence. Be prepared to explain what each piece represents and how it supports your case. Keep your explanations concise and relevant.

Choosing and Preparing Witnesses
1. Who Makes a Good Witness?

Strong witnesses can provide firsthand accounts of your parenting and your child's relationship with you. Consider these options:

- **Family Members:** Relatives who have observed your involvement in your child's life.
- **Teachers or Coaches:** Educators or mentors who can speak about your role in supporting your child's education or activities.
- **Healthcare Providers:** Doctors or therapists who can vouch for your attention to your child's health and well-being.

- **Childcare Providers:** Babysitters or daycare workers who have seen you interact with your child.

2. Prepare Your Witnesses:

Before the hearing, meet with your witnesses to review what they'll say. They should focus on factual observations rather than opinions. For example, a teacher might describe how you regularly attend parent-teacher conferences rather than stating, "He's a better parent."

3. Be Honest About Witness Testimonies:

Avoid pressuring witnesses to exaggerate or lie. Courts value credibility, and dishonest testimony can harm your case.

4. Ensure They Are Available:

Check your witnesses' schedules to ensure they can attend the hearing. If someone cannot attend in person, ask the court about alternative options, such as written statements or virtual testimony.

Presenting Evidence and Witnesses in Court

1. Follow Court Procedures:

Courts have specific rules for introducing evidence and witnesses. Work with your lawyer to ensure you follow these procedures. For example, some courts require you to formally "enter" evidence into the record before discussing it.

2. Be Clear and Professional:

When presenting evidence, be clear about what each piece represents and why it matters. Avoid emotional language or lengthy explanations.

3. Support Witness Testimonies with Evidence:

Whenever possible, back up a witness's testimony with physical evidence. For instance, if a teacher says you're actively involved in your child's education, you might provide copies of report cards or notes from school meetings to support their statement.

4. Be Prepared for Cross-Examination:

The other parent's lawyer may question your witnesses to challenge their credibility. Ensure your witnesses know to stay calm and answer questions truthfully.

Common Mistakes to Avoid

1. Submitting Irrelevant Evidence:

When preparing your custody case, focus on gathering evidence that directly supports your argument. Submitting too many irrelevant items can dilute the impact of your key points and may even frustrate the court.

2. Overloading the Court:

More isn't always better. Present a manageable amount of evidence that highlights your strengths.

3. Failing to Prepare Witnesses:

Unprepared witnesses may stumble over questions or appear unreliable. Take time to review their testimony with them beforehand.

4. Appearing Overly Defensive:

Stick to the facts and avoid getting defensive during cross-examination. Calm, respectful behavior makes a strong impression.

Strategic Suggestions

- **Start Early:** Begin gathering evidence and identifying witnesses as soon as your custody case begins.
- **Work Closely with Your Lawyer:** A custody lawyer can guide you on what evidence to present and how to prepare witnesses effectively.
- **Stay Focused on the Child:** Frame all evidence and testimony around what's best for your child, not your personal grievances with the other parent.
- **Maintain a Professional Demeanor:** Your behavior in court matters as much as the evidence you present. Stay respectful and composed at all times.

Presenting evidence and witnesses effectively can strengthen your custody case significantly. With preparation, organization, and a focus on your child's well-being, you can use this opportunity to demonstrate your commitment and capabilities as a parent.

Chapter 7: Handling Mediation and Negotiation

Handling mediation and negotiation involves working collaboratively with the other parent to reach agreements on custody and parenting plans. This process is important for minimizing conflict and creating solutions that prioritize your child's needs. Effective communication and preparation can lead to fair, sustainable outcomes while maintaining a respectful co-parenting relationship.

Preparing for Mediation Sessions

Mediation can be one of the most effective tools in resolving custody issues without the emotional and financial strain of a court battle. During mediation, you and the other parent will meet with a neutral third party, known as the mediator, to discuss and potentially reach agreements on custody and visitation matters.

Why Mediation Matters

Mediation is an opportunity for both parents to express their concerns and work toward a solution that prioritizes the child's well-being. It often sets the tone for how parents communicate and cooperate moving forward.

Steps to Prepare for Mediation

1. Understand the Mediation Process

Before your session, take time to learn how mediation works. Typically, it involves:

- A brief introduction from the mediator explaining their role and the ground rules.
- Each parent presenting their perspective on custody and visitation.
- A guided discussion to identify common ground and resolve disagreements.

The mediator will not make decisions for you; their role is to facilitate productive conversations and help you reach a mutual agreement.

2. Know Your Goals

Think carefully about what you want to achieve in mediation. Consider:

- The type of custody arrangement you believe is best for your child (joint custody, physical custody, etc.).
- A visitation schedule that works for both parents and supports your child's routine.

- Any specific needs your child has, such as schooling, healthcare, or extracurricular activities.

Write down these goals and prioritize them so you can clearly communicate your desires during mediation.

3. Gather Supporting Information

Come prepared with facts and evidence that support your position. This could include:

- A calendar showing how much time you've spent with your child.
- Documentation of your involvement in your child's education, healthcare, and activities.
- Notes about your work schedule and availability for parenting responsibilities.

4. Anticipate the Other Parent's Concerns

Think about what the other parent might request or argue during mediation. Being prepared to address their concerns calmly and respectfully can improve your chances of finding common ground.

For example, if the other parent worries about your work hours affecting visitation, you could suggest solutions like adjusting your schedule or involving a trusted family member to help with transitions.

Communicating Effectively During Mediation

1. Stay Focused on the Child:

Always frame your points around what benefits your child the most. Avoid criticizing the other parent or making the discussion about your personal grievances.

2. Be Respectful and Cooperative

Mediation works best when both parents approach it with a willingness to collaborate. Stay calm and respectful, even if tensions rise. If you find yourself getting frustrated, take a deep breath and refocus on your child's needs.

3. Use Clear and Specific Language:

Ambiguity can lead to misunderstandings later. Be as specific as possible when discussing schedules, responsibilities, or expectations.

Mistakes to Avoid in Mediation

1. Being Unprepared

Failing to plan ahead can make you appear disorganized or uninterested in your child's well-being. Take time to think through your goals and gather relevant information.

2. Letting Emotions Take Over

Custody discussions can be emotional, but it's important to stay composed. Focus on facts and solutions rather than getting caught up in arguments or blame.

3. Refusing to Compromise

Mediation requires give-and-take from both sides. Be prepared to make reasonable concessions in exchange for agreements that meet your priorities.

4. Ignoring Legal Advice

Consult your lawyer before mediation to ensure your proposals align with legal standards and protect your rights.

5. After the Mediation Session

Once the mediation session ends, you'll likely leave with a draft agreement or a list of unresolved issues to address later. Review any agreements carefully, preferably with your lawyer, before signing. Ensure that the terms are fair, clear, and in your child's best interests.

Strategic Suggestions

- **Practice Active Listening:** Make an effort to truly hear what the other parent and the mediator are saying. Acknowledging their concerns can build goodwill and foster cooperation.
- **Stay Flexible:** Be willing to explore creative solutions that balance both parents' needs and schedules.

- **Keep the Child's Perspective in Mind:** Regularly ask yourself, "How does this benefit my child?" This mindset helps you stay focused on what truly matters.
- **Follow Up Thoroughly:** If agreements are made, ensure they are finalized promptly and implemented effectively.

Mediation can be a powerful tool for resolving custody matters without prolonged conflict. Prepare thoroughly and approaching the process with a positive and cooperative attitude to work toward an arrangement that benefits your child and fosters healthy co-parenting.

Negotiating Custody and Visitation Agreements

Negotiating custody and visitation agreements is often one of the most challenging yet critical parts of the custody process. It's an opportunity for both parents to create a plan that supports the child's well-being while respecting each parent's role. Successful negotiations require preparation, clarity, and a focus on cooperation.

Understanding Custody and Visitation Agreements

A custody and visitation agreement outlines where the child will live, how time will be shared between parents, and how decisions about the child will be made. There are two primary components:

1. Custody

This includes legal custody (decision-making authority) and physical custody (where the child resides).

2. Visitation

This specifies the schedule for when the non-custodial parent will spend time with the child.

The goal of negotiations is to create a plan that minimizes conflict and maximizes stability for your child.

Steps for Successful Negotiation

1. Prioritize Your Child's Needs

The foundation of any custody agreement should be the child's best interests. Think about their daily routine, emotional needs, and educational requirements. Acknowledge what's most important for their development, even if it requires compromises.

For example:

- Does your child need consistency in their school or extracurricular schedule?
- Are they more comfortable having one primary residence or splitting time equally between parents?

By centering the conversation on your child, you demonstrate your commitment to their well-being.

2. Know What You Want Before Negotiations Begin

Prepare a detailed plan outlining your ideal custody and visitation arrangement. Include specifics such as:

- Weekly schedules (e.g., weekdays, weekends, holidays).
- Transportation responsibilities.
- Arrangements for special occasions (e.g., birthdays, vacations).

Having a clear plan ensures you can articulate your preferences confidently during negotiations.

3. Be Willing to Compromise:

Flexibility is key to reaching an agreement. Be open to alternative arrangements that still meet your core goals. For example:

- If the other parent wants more weekday time, propose extended weekend visits to balance the schedule.
- If both parents work full-time, consider involving trusted family members or childcare services to bridge gaps.

4. Document Your Involvement

Supporting your position with evidence of your active parenting can strengthen your case. Examples include:

- Records of attendance at school events, medical appointments, or extracurricular activities.
- Communication logs showing consistent effort to co-parent effectively.
- A calendar of time already spent with your child.

5. Keep Emotions in Check

Custody negotiations can be emotional, but it's essential to stay calm and focused. Avoid letting anger or frustration derail the discussion.

Instead, use respectful language and listen to the other parent's perspective.

Key Elements to Include in the Agreement

1. Custody Designation

Clearly define whether you're seeking joint custody, sole custody, or a combination. Specify how decision-making responsibilities will be divided.

2. Visitation Schedule

Create a detailed calendar that includes:

- Regular weekly schedules.
- Plans for holidays, birthdays, and vacations.
- Provisions for last-minute changes or emergencies.

3. Communication Guidelines

Set expectations for how you and the other parent will communicate about the child. This could include using co-parenting apps or scheduling regular check-ins.

4. Dispute Resolution Plan

Agreeing on a clear method for resolving future conflicts, such as mediation or involving a parenting coordinator, is an essential step in co-parenting effectively. This proactive approach helps prevent small disagreements from escalating into bigger disputes that could negatively affect your child.

Common Pitfalls to Avoid

1. Making It About Winning:

Custody is not about beating the other parent. Focus on creating an arrangement that benefits your child, not one that "proves a point."

2. Ignoring Practical Logistics:

Be realistic about your schedule and responsibilities. For example, don't agree to weekday custody if your work hours conflict with school pick-ups and drop-offs.

3. Overlooking Future Needs

Children's needs change as they grow. Build flexibility into the agreement to accommodate future adjustments.

4. Forgetting to Consult Your Lawyer

Run any proposed agreement by your lawyer before finalizing it. They can ensure the terms protect your rights and align with legal standards.

After the Agreement Is Reached

Once you've negotiated an agreement, review it carefully with your attorney. Ensure every detail is clear and enforceable. Then, submit it to the court for approval. Court approval makes the agreement legally binding and helps prevent future disputes.

Strategic Suggestions

- **Stay Child-Centered:** Regularly ask yourself, "Is this what's best for my child?" This perspective keeps discussions constructive.

- **Leverage Professional Support:** Consider involving a mediator or parenting coordinator to facilitate discussions and reduce tension.

- **Be Proactive About Problem-Solving:** Anticipate potential conflicts (e.g., holiday scheduling) and address them in the agreement to avoid future issues.

- **Maintain Open Communication:** Keeping lines of communication open after negotiations can help both parents adhere to the agreement and resolve minor disputes amicably.

Negotiating custody and visitation agreements is a collaborative process. With preparation, patience, and a focus on your child's well-being, you can create a plan that supports a healthy co-parenting relationship and provides stability for your child.

Resolving Disputes Without Court Intervention

When disputes arise during custody proceedings or co-parenting, finding solutions outside the courtroom is often better for everyone involved, especially the child. Court battles can be time-consuming, expensive, and emotionally draining. Taking proactive steps to resolve disagreements through alternative methods fosters cooperation and creates a healthier environment for your child.

Why Avoid Court for Custody Disputes?

While court intervention may seem like the quickest way to settle disagreements, it's rarely ideal. Here's why:

1. Cost

Legal fees and court expenses can add up quickly, burdening both parents financially.

2. Time

Court cases can take months or even years to resolve, prolonging stress for you and your child.

3. Stress on the Child

Watching their parents battle in court can negatively impact a child's emotional well-being.

4. Loss of Control

Judges make the final decision in court, and it may not align with what either parent truly wants.

Resolving disputes outside of court helps you maintain control over the outcome while prioritizing your child's stability.

Effective Methods for Dispute Resolution

1. Open Communication

The first step in addressing any disagreement is open and honest communication with the other parent. While emotions may run high, try to keep discussions respectful and focused on solutions.

- **Use a neutral tones:** Avoid accusatory language. For example, say, "How can we make this schedule work better for both of us?" instead of, "You're always making things difficult."
- **Stick to the topic:** Stay focused on the issue at hand and avoid bringing up past grievances.

If direct conversations are challenging, consider using co-parenting communication apps like OurFamilyWizard or Talking Parents. These platforms structure conversations and reduce misunderstandings.

2. Mediation

Mediation involves a neutral third party who facilitates discussions between you and the other parent. The mediator helps both parties identify common ground and work toward a mutually acceptable solution.

Benefits of mediation

- It's less formal and intimidating than court.
- It encourages cooperation and compromise.
- It's confidential, unlike court proceedings.

Most courts encourage or even require mediation before escalating custody disputes to trial, so it's a step worth pursuing.

3. Parenting Coordinators

If disputes are frequent or communication is particularly strained, a parenting coordinator can be invaluable. This professional helps parents resolve ongoing conflicts, implement parenting plans, and make decisions in the child's best interest.

When to consider a parenting coordinator

- If you and the other parent have difficulty following the custody agreement.

- If disagreements repeatedly disrupt your co-parenting arrangement.

4. Collaborative Law

Collaborative law is an alternative dispute resolution process where both parents, along with their lawyers, commit to resolving the dispute without going to court. Everyone works together to reach an agreement that satisfies both parties.

Key features

- Open sharing of information.
- A commitment to avoid litigation.
- Focused discussions led by legal professionals and other experts (e.g., child psychologists).

This approach works well when both parents are genuinely committed to cooperation.

5. Counseling or Therapy

Sometimes, custody disputes stem from unresolved personal conflicts or misunderstandings about co-parenting roles. Family counseling or therapy can provide tools for better communication and conflict resolution. A trained therapist can:

- Help parents separate personal grievances from parenting issues.
- Offer strategies to reduce tension during interactions.

6. Compromise and Creativity

When disputes arise, don't be afraid to think outside the box. Sometimes, unconventional solutions can satisfy both parents' needs while prioritizing the child. For example:

- If weekends are a point of contention, consider alternating long weekends (Friday to Monday) instead of traditional two-day schedules.
- If vacations are an issue, agree on a set number of flexible days each parent can use annually, with notice.

Preventing Future Disputes

Resolving disputes is essential, but preventing them is even better. Take these steps to minimize conflict:

1. Create a Detailed Parenting Plan

Address as many potential scenarios as possible upfront. This includes holidays, vacations, and emergency situations.

2. Establish Clear Boundaries

Define how you'll handle communication, decision-making, and schedule changes.

3. Be Flexible When Necessary

While consistency is crucial for your child, occasional adjustments may be needed. Being adaptable shows goodwill and reduces animosity.

4. Focus on the Bigger Picture

Custody battles and co-parenting challenges can sometimes make emotions run high, but focusing on what's best for your child helps you navigate these situations with clarity and compassion.

Handling Difficult Situations

Despite your best efforts, some disputes may be particularly challenging to resolve. In such cases, it's essential to:

1. Stay Calm

Avoid reacting impulsively or escalating the conflict.

2. Document Everything

Keep records of conversations, agreements, and incidents that may influence the resolution process.

3. Seek Professional Guidance

Don't hesitate to consult your lawyer, a mediator, or a therapist if you're struggling to find a solution.

Strategic Suggestions

- **Build a Problem-Solving Mindset:** Approach disputes with the mindset that both parents can win if the solution benefits the child.

- **Prioritize Neutral Spaces:** Conduct discussions in neutral locations, like a mediator's office, to keep emotions in check.
- **Focus on Long-Term Cooperation:** Remember that resolving disputes amicably builds trust and strengthens your co-parenting relationship.
- **Educate Yourself About Resources:** Familiarize yourself with available tools like parenting coordinators, co-parenting apps, and local mediation services.

Resolving disputes without court intervention requires patience, empathy, and a commitment to compromise. When parents work together to find solutions, they create a more harmonious environment for their child and lay the groundwork for successful co-parenting.

Chapter 8: Ensuring a Positive Image

Ensuring a positive image means presenting yourself as a responsible and caring parent through your actions and behavior. This is essential for influencing how others perceive your ability to provide for your child's well-being. Maintaining composure, professionalism, and integrity strengthens your case and supports your role as a reliable caregiver.

Maintaining Good Behavior During the Custody Process

When you're going through a custody battle, it's crucial to maintain a positive and composed behavior. Your actions and attitude during this process will influence how the court and others perceive you as a parent. Custody decisions are ultimately about the best interests of your child, and demonstrating that you can remain calm, responsible, and considerate throughout the proceedings can strengthen your case.

The Importance of Setting a Positive Example

During a custody case, every move you make could be scrutinized, and any negative behavior can be used against you. But it's not just about avoiding mistakes—it's also about showing that you're capable of being a supportive, stable, and caring parent. How you handle the custody process can have a significant impact on the court's perception of your parenting ability.

Here's why maintaining good behavior is so important:

1. Court's Focus on Parental Responsibility

Judges want to know that both parents can take responsibility for their child's physical and emotional needs. The way you behave during the process determines your ability to meet these needs.

2. Stable Environment for the Child

The court will consider how the child will be affected by the custody arrangement. If you are emotionally balanced and behave responsibly, it shows the judge that you can provide the stability your child needs.

3. Impact on the Child's Well-being

Your behavior influences not only the court's decision but also your child's emotional state.

Children are very sensitive to tension, so being mindful of your conduct can protect their mental and emotional well-being.

How to Maintain Good Behavior
1. Be Respectful Toward the Other Parent

Even if you're angry or frustrated with your ex, maintaining respect in front of the judge and others is key. Avoid bad-mouthing your ex to your child or in court.

- **Keep communication neutral and civil:** Stick to facts and issues that directly relate to your child's well-being.
- **Focus on what's best for the child:** Always keep the child's interests as the priority when discussing or interacting with your ex.

2. Be Present for Your Child

Actions speak louder than words. Showing up for your child, not just physically but emotionally, sends a strong message to the court that you're dedicated to your child's happiness and stability.

- **Attend important events:** Be there for your child during school meetings, sports activities, or doctor appointments. These actions demonstrate that you're involved and care about your child's life and well-being.
- **Provide emotional support:** Show your child love, patience, and encouragement. Even though you're going through a stressful time, your child should see you as a steady, supportive presence.

3. Avoid Arguments in Front of the Children

Custody disputes can be stressful, but it's crucial to keep your disagreements out of your child's earshot. Children are often caught in the middle of their parents' issues, which can make them feel anxious, sad, or guilty.

- **Keep conflict private:** If you need to have a difficult conversation, do it away from the children.
- **Create a peaceful environment:** Make sure your home is a safe, nurturing place where your child feels secure. Avoid raising your voice or having heated discussions where your child can overhear.

4. Be Consistent with Parenting Responsibilities

One of the key factors in any custody case is the ability to provide a consistent and stable environment for the child. If you have parenting duties, take them seriously. Show that you are capable of managing your responsibilities.

- **Follow your parenting plan:** Adhere to the visitation schedules, school routines, and any other agreed-upon rules.

- **Follow through with commitments:** If you promised your child something, make sure you deliver. This will demonstrate that you can be relied upon as a parent.

5. Stay Calm During the Legal Process

The legal process can be long and frustrating. However, it's important to stay calm and not let emotions drive your actions.

- **Avoid engaging in drama:** Don't allow yourself to get caught up in unnecessary arguments or negative exchanges.
- **Stay composed in court:** If you're in a courtroom setting, remain calm and respectful. Stick to the facts, and avoid being defensive or confrontational.

6. Take Care of Your Personal Well-being

You can't be a strong parent if you're struggling with your own emotional or physical well-being.

It's important to take care of yourself so you can be there for your child.

- **Manage stress:** Find healthy ways to cope with stress through exercise, meditation, or talking to a friend.
- **Seek professional support:** If you're finding it difficult to manage emotions or mental health issues, don't hesitate to seek support from a therapist or counselor.

The Impact of Your Behavior on the Custody Case

The court will not only evaluate your actions but also how well you manage the stress of the custody process. Maintaining good behavior can give the court confidence in your ability to co-parent effectively and create a positive environment for your child.

Your behavior is crucial, especially when the other parent is also making a case for custody. A consistent, respectful, and cooperative approach will help you stand out as a committed father who is putting the child's needs first.

Strategic Suggestions

- **Stay Calm and Collected:** If you're dealing with the other parent, legal representatives, or the court system, keeping your cool will go a long way in showing your maturity and commitment.
- **Be a Role Model for Your Child:** Demonstrate kindness, responsibility, and patience to set a positive example for your child.
- **Create Positive Memories:** Focus on quality time with your child. This not only strengthens your bond but also reinforces your image as an engaged and loving parent.
- **Document Your Efforts:** Keep a record of your involvement in your child's life, such as appointments you attend, school activities, and other meaningful interactions. This can be

useful to show your commitment to your child's well-being.

Stay positive, show maturity, and demonstrate your dedication to your child's best interests to strengthen your position in the custody battle. Your behavior throughout the process will ultimately show that you're not just fighting for custody, but for the long-term happiness and stability of your child.

Managing Social Media and Public Perception

In today's digital age, your social media activity and how you present yourself online can play a surprising role in a custody battle. Social media provides a platform for sharing personal opinions, moments, and photos, but it can also lead to unintended consequences if not carefully managed. Your posts can be viewed by your ex-partner, potential witnesses, the court, or anyone connected to your case. It's crucial to understand how to manage your online presence to ensure that it supports your position as a responsible and loving parent.

The Importance of Being Cautious with Social Media

Social media can be a double-edged sword during a custody battle. What may seem like an innocent post can be used as evidence against you. Negative or careless posts could suggest that you're not as committed to your child's best interests as you claim. Moreover, your posts might inadvertently affect the way others perceive you.

Here's how social media can impact your custody case:

1. Evidence in Court

Posts, photos, and comments from your social media accounts can be used as evidence during your case. If you make controversial, inappropriate, or angry posts about your ex or your situation, these can be introduced in court to question your behavior and judgment.

2. Public Perception

The way you portray yourself online could shape how others—potential witnesses or even the judge—see you. If you appear to be hostile, irresponsible, or unstable online, it can hurt your case.

3. Impact on Your Child's Well-being

Your child may eventually come across these posts, which could affect their emotional well-being. Posting negative or overly personal content about the custody battle could be confusing and upsetting for your child.

How to Manage Your Social Media During a Custody Battle

1. Be Mindful of What You Post

Every post you make maybe it is a picture, status update, or comment, could be seen by someone involved in your case.

- **Avoid posting about the custody case:** It's crucial to keep details about your case off social media. Don't air grievances or talk about the process online.
- **Think before sharing personal information:** Posting about your child's activities or your personal struggles can inadvertently bring unwanted attention to your case. Be

mindful of how much you're revealing to the public.

- **Refrain from venting or criticizing:** Venting about your ex or the legal process can make you appear vindictive or unstable. If you need to express your feelings, do so privately, away from the public eye.

2. Set Your Accounts to Private

While nothing on the internet is ever completely private, you can minimize exposure by adjusting your privacy settings.

- **Adjust privacy settings:** Make sure your profiles are set to private, so only people you trust can see your posts.
- **Be selective with friend requests:** Avoid adding anyone involved in the case or potential witnesses. It's best to limit your social media connections to close family and friends who understand your situation.

- **Review your posts regularly:** Even with private settings, old posts can still be found and potentially used against you. Go through your past posts and remove anything that could be seen in a negative light.

3. Don't Post Negative Comments About Your Ex

While it can be tempting to express your frustration about the other parent, public displays of negativity will only harm your case.

- **Avoid name-calling or insults:** Refrain from posting anything derogatory about your ex or their actions. Even if your ex is being difficult, avoid engaging in an online argument.
- **Stick to facts:** If you must discuss anything related to your ex, keep it neutral and stick to facts. Avoid emotional language that can paint you as hostile or vengeful.

4. Be Mindful of Photos and Videos

The photos and videos you post can also be used to support or undermine your case.

- **Think carefully about what you share:** Avoid posting images that could be seen as irresponsible, unsafe, or inappropriate. For example, avoid posting photos that show reckless behavior, excessive drinking, or anything that could raise concerns about your parenting abilities.
- **Limit what you share about your child:** While it's natural to want to share moments with your child, ensure that the images and details you share are appropriate and respectful.

5. Monitor Your Ex's Social Media

While it's essential to control your own online presence, it's also worth keeping an eye on what your ex is posting.

- **Stay informed:** If your ex is posting things that could affect your case, such as inappropriate behavior or false information, it could be helpful to keep a record of these posts.
- **Avoid reacting publicly:** If your ex posts something that is harmful to you, refrain from responding in a public forum. A calm and composed response, possibly through your lawyer, is far more effective than engaging in an online argument.

How to Handle Public Perception

Consider how your actions and interactions in public may be perceived. Public perception is important because the court, your ex, and others may form an opinion about you based on how you conduct yourself outside the courtroom.

- **Maintain professionalism and civility:** If you're interacting with your ex in person or communicating with others about the case, always maintain a respectful tone. This demonstrates that you are capable of handling difficult situations with maturity.

Avoid making inflammatory comments: In conversations with friends or family, avoid speaking ill of your ex or the custody battle. This could be used against you as evidence that you're not a team player in the co-parenting process.

Strategic Suggestions

- **Keep Your Social Media Accounts Clean:** Only post content that is positive, respectful, and neutral. Avoid anything that might reflect poorly on you as a parent or individual.
- **Keep Personal Details Private:** Be cautious about sharing too much personal information, especially if it pertains to the custody case.
- **Monitor Your Ex's Online Activity:** Stay aware of what your ex is posting, but refrain from engaging publicly. If

necessary, consult your lawyer about how to address any damaging posts.

- **Engage in Positive Offline Activities:** Focus on maintaining a positive reputation offline as well. Volunteer, participate in community activities, and engage in hobbies that reflect your commitment to being a responsible parent.

Carefully manage your online presence and being mindful of public perceptions to help build a strong, positive image during your custody battle. Social media and public interactions are an extension of your behavior in the legal process, so keeping them aligned with your parenting goals will only strengthen your case.

Addressing Allegations and Misunderstandings

During a custody battle, accusations can sometimes arise due to misunderstandings, miscommunications, or deliberate efforts to damage your reputation. These allegations can range from minor misunderstandings to more serious claims of neglect or abuse. Regardless of the nature of the accusations, it's important to handle them calmly and strategically.

Types of Allegations You May Face

There are several types of allegations that may arise in a custody battle. Understanding what they are can help you prepare to address them effectively:

1. Allegations of Abuse or Neglect

These are among the most serious accusations a parent can face, and they can have a huge impact on your custody case. These allegations could be based on concerns about your ability to care for your child.

2. Claims of Substance Abuse or Addiction

If your ex or someone involved in the case claims that you have substance abuse problems, this could significantly affect your chances of gaining custody or visitation rights.

3. Claims of Inadequate Parenting

Allegations may be made regarding your parenting style, including claims that you aren't actively involved in your child's life, or that you are neglecting their emotional or physical needs.

4. Claims of Poor Living Conditions

If it's alleged that you're not providing a safe or stable living environment for your child, it could raise concerns about your parenting.

5. False Accusations of Alienation

In some cases, one parent may accuse the other of trying to alienate the child from them, which could lead to questions about your motives and behavior.

How to Respond to Allegations

1. Stay Calm and Avoid Reacting Emotionally

First and foremost, it's crucial that you stay calm when confronted with allegations. Reacting impulsively or angrily can give the impression that you have something to hide or that you're incapable of controlling your emotions. Instead, take a step back and approach the situation rationally.

- **Don't argue in public:** If the allegation is made by your ex or their lawyer in public or in court, remain composed. Responding in front of others could make the situation worse.
- **Take time to process:** If you hear about an allegation, take some time to process the information before responding. You may want to consult

with your attorney about how to handle the situation.

2. Document Everything

One of the most important steps you can take in addressing allegations is to keep detailed records. Your documentation will serve as evidence that supports your side of the story and helps refute any false claims.

- **Keep a written record:** Document any interactions or communications that relate to the allegation. This could include emails, text messages, and notes on conversations. If your ex or anyone else is making accusations, having a detailed timeline and records of events can be incredibly helpful.
- **Gather supporting evidence:** If the allegation involves an incident (e.g., accusations of neglect or abuse), try to gather any evidence that supports your version of the events. This could include

medical records, witness statements, or even photos.

- **Stay organized:** Keep all of your records neatly organized in a folder, either physical or digital, for easy access when needed in court.

3. Address False Accusations Head-On

If the allegations made against you are false, it's important to address them directly. Your response should be clear, factual, and based on evidence.

- **Stick to the facts:** When defending yourself against false accusations, always focus on the facts. Avoid making personal attacks or emotional arguments. Instead, present any evidence that disproves the claims made against you.
- **Consult with your attorney:** Your lawyer will help you craft a response and determine how best to present the evidence in your favor. If needed, your

lawyer can also help you prepare to cross-examine the person who made the allegation.

- **Refute misinformation:** If an allegation is based on incorrect information, such as a misunderstanding or a misinterpreted event, be sure to clarify the facts. Provide context for the situation and explain the misunderstanding.

4. Demonstrate Your Commitment to Your Child's Well-being

Regardless of the nature of the allegations, it's essential that you consistently demonstrate your commitment to your child's best interests. Show the court that you are a loving, responsible, and involved parent.

- **Be proactive:** Take steps to show that you are doing everything in your power to care for your child's physical, emotional, and psychological needs. This could include enrolling your child in extracurricular activities, attending school events, or keeping up with doctor's appointments.

- **Stay involved:** Regularly communicate with your child's school, teachers, and other important figures in their life. This will demonstrate that you are an active part of your child's world and dedicated to their success.
- **Show stability:** If your ex is accusing you of being unstable, ensure that you can demonstrate your own stability. This can include maintaining steady employment, living in a safe environment, and having a structured routine for your child.

5. Focus on the Big Picture

While dealing with allegations may feel overwhelming in the moment, remember to keep your focus on the big picture. The goal is to show the court that you are a fit parent who deserves time with your child.

- **Don't get sidetracked by petty accusations:** Sometimes, allegations are made to provoke you or to distract from the real issue at hand. Avoid getting bogged down in irrelevant details. Focus on your ability to provide a stable, loving environment for your child.
- **Stay focused on the best interests of your child:** At all times, ensure that your actions and responses prioritize your child's needs and well-being. This will reflect positively on your character in court.

Strategic Suggestions

- **Stay Calm:** Even if the allegations are false or upsetting, keeping a calm and rational approach is crucial to your credibility.
- **Document Everything:** Always keep thorough records of communications,

incidents, and evidence that supports your case.

- **Work with Your Attorney:** Consult with your lawyer immediately when allegations arise to determine the best course of action.
- **Refute False Claims with Evidence:** When accusations are unfounded, present the facts and any supporting evidence to disprove them.
- **Keep Your Focus on the Child's Best Interests:** Throughout the process, maintain a focus on what is best for your child, demonstrating your ability to provide a safe and nurturing environment.

Handling allegations and misunderstandings in a custody battle requires composure, preparation, and a strategic approach. Address accusations promptly and provide the right documentation and evidence, so you protect your chances for a positive outcome.

Chapter 9: Supporting Your Child During the Process

Supporting your child during the process means providing emotional stability, reassurance, and understanding as they navigate changes in their family dynamic. This is essential for minimizing stress and helping them feel secure. Stay attentive to their needs and maintain open communication, so you can protect their well-being and strengthen your bond.

Communicating the Situation to Your Child

When going through a custody battle, one of the most sensitive aspects is how to communicate the situation to your child. This is a time of uncertainty and stress, not only for you but for your child as well. Children often feel confused, anxious, and torn between their parents, especially if they are old enough to understand that things are changing. It's essential to approach the situation thoughtfully, keeping in mind that the way you communicate with your child can have a lasting impact on their emotional well-being.

When to Have the Conversation

Deciding when to talk to your child about the custody battle is crucial. The timing will depend on your child's age, maturity level, and understanding of the situation. Generally, it's best to have the conversation when you are sure that the custody proceedings are going to affect their daily life, such as a change in where they live, visitation schedules, or how often they see each parent.

For younger children, it might not be necessary to go into great detail about the specifics of the legal process. Instead, focus on the changes they will notice in their day-to-day life. Older children, however, may have more questions and might already be aware of what's going on, so it's important to address their concerns honestly.

How to Approach the Conversation

When you speak to your child about the custody process, there are a few key principles to keep in mind:

1. Be Honest, But Age-Appropriate

The level of detail you provide should match your child's age and understanding. For younger children, it may be enough to explain that sometimes parents don't live together anymore, but they will still be loved and taken care of. For older children, you can explain the reasons behind the changes, but avoid going into adult details. You don't need to overshare, especially about the reasons for the divorce or any conflicts with the other parent. Children should feel reassured that they are not to blame for the situation.

2. Keep It Positive

Try to frame the conversation in a way that focuses on stability and security. Emphasize that both parents love them and want to ensure that they continue to have a relationship with both. Even though the situation may feel uncertain, make sure your child understands that both parents will be working together to make things work for them.

3. Reassure Your Child

The most important thing during this time is to offer your child reassurance. Explain that it's normal for families to go through changes, and while things may feel different, they are still safe, loved, and supported. Children need to feel secure, so avoid any language that might make them feel responsible for the divorce or custody battle. Make sure they know it's not their fault.

4. Encourage Questions

Allow your child to express their feelings and ask questions. They may not always ask immediately, but let them know they can talk to you whenever they need. Be prepared to answer their questions honestly, even if the answers are difficult or uncomfortable. If you don't know the answer to a question, be honest about it. It's okay to say, "I don't know yet, but I will let you know as soon as I do."

5. Don't Criticize the Other Parent

Even if you are going through a tough time with the other parent, try to keep your opinions and frustrations to yourself when speaking to your child. Avoid saying anything negative about the other parent. Children need to feel that both parents are still important parts of their lives.

Criticizing the other parent can make your child feel like they have to choose sides, which can increase their stress.

6. Use Reassuring Body Language and Tone

Your child will be looking to you for emotional cues, so your body language and tone of voice are just as important as your words. Speak calmly and with confidence to assure them that everything will be okay. Your demeanor should be open and approachable, making it clear that your child can come to you with any concerns.

What to Expect After the Conversation

After the conversation, your child might experience a variety of emotions. They may feel sad, confused, or even angry. It's normal for children to have questions or emotional reactions, so be prepared for this. You may need to revisit the conversation more than once as they process the changes in their lives. This is why it's important to continue offering reassurance and making yourself available to talk.

If your child seems particularly upset or struggles with the situation, it might be helpful to seek support from a counselor or therapist. Children often benefit from having a neutral person to talk to, especially during such a stressful time. Additionally, a therapist can help your child develop coping strategies and provide you with tips on how to help them manage their emotions.

Strategic Suggestions

- **Create a Support System:** Surround your child with a strong support system, including trusted family members or friends who can provide emotional support.
- **Monitor Changes in Behavior:** Keep an eye out for any behavioral changes in your child. Signs of stress or anxiety might include changes in sleeping or eating patterns, withdrawal, or trouble

concentrating. If you notice these signs, seek professional help.

- **Maintain Open Communication:** Regularly check in with your child. Let them know that their feelings are valid and that it's okay to talk about what's going on. Reassure them that you are there for them.
- **Don't Force It:** If your child isn't ready to talk or asks not to discuss it, respect their space. However, always make sure they know they can come to you when they are ready.

Communicating with your child during a custody battle can be challenging, but it's also one of the most important things you can do. Being honest, calm, and supportive will help your child feel secure, loved, and understood. It's essential to keep the conversation open and ongoing as your child processes the changes happening in their life.

Prioritizing Emotional and Mental Well-Being

Going through a custody battle is a stressful and emotionally taxing experience—not just for you as a parent, but for your child as well. The process can create a lot of uncertainty and tension, which may take a toll on everyone's emotional and mental health. It is important that you prioritize both your well-being and your child's during this challenging time. Focusing on emotional stability can help you manage the stress of the situation while also ensuring that your child feels supported and secure.

Recognizing the Emotional Impact on Your Child

The emotional impact of a custody battle on your child can vary depending on their age, temperament, and understanding of the situation. Younger children might not fully grasp what's going on but can still sense tension, anxiety, or changes in their environment. Older children, however, are more likely to be directly affected by the custody proceedings and may have a better understanding of what's happening, especially if they are asked to share their own preferences with the court.

Your child may experience a range of emotions such as:

1. Confusion and Anxiety

Your child may feel unsettled by the changes to their routine, living arrangements, and relationships with both parents. This is especially true if they are used to one parent being more involved or living together as a family.

2. Sadness or Grief

Many children mourn the loss of the family structure they were once familiar with. The divorce or custody process can make them feel like something important is being taken away from them.

3. Anger or Frustration

Some children might act out or become angry, especially if they feel powerless in the situation. They may also feel frustration over being put in the middle or pressured to take sides.

4. Guilt

Children sometimes blame themselves for the divorce or custody issues, even though the situation is not their fault. They might believe that their behavior caused the separation or that they are responsible for making their parents happy.

Understanding that these feelings are normal will help you navigate the emotional complexities of the process.

How to Prioritize Emotional Well-Being

Taking care of your child's emotional health is essential during this time. As a parent, you are your child's primary source of emotional support, and how you react to the custody battle will significantly influence their well-being. Here are several strategies you can use to help prioritize their emotional health:

1. Create Stability and Routine

Children find comfort in routine, especially during times of uncertainty. Try to maintain a sense of normalcy in your child's day-to-day life. Keep regular bedtimes, meal times, and activities. If possible, try to avoid making significant changes to their environment or routine until they've had time to adjust to the situation. Stability can be a grounding force for children, making them feel more secure and less anxious.

2. Listen and Acknowledge Their Feelings

Allow your child to express their emotions, and listen without judgment. Validate their feelings by acknowledging that it's okay for them to feel upset, sad, or confused. Reassure them that you understand and that their feelings are normal.

Sometimes, just knowing that they have someone to talk to can provide a great deal of comfort.

3. Be a Source of Calm

Children often look to their parents for cues on how to respond to stressful situations. It's important to model calmness and resilience, even if you're feeling stressed or anxious yourself. Children are more likely to feel secure when they see their parents maintaining a sense of control. Speak to your child in a gentle, reassuring voice and avoid raising your voice or displaying frustration. The more you show emotional stability, the more likely your child will feel at ease.

4. Offer Reassurance and Affection

Reassure your child that, despite the changes, they are still loved and important to both parents. Offer plenty of physical affection, such as hugs or holding hands. This can be especially comforting for younger children who may have trouble expressing their emotions with words. For older children, verbal reassurance and showing interest in their lives can help them feel valued and supported.

5. Seek Professional Support If Needed

If your child is struggling with their emotions, consider seeking the help of a child therapist or counselor. A mental health professional can provide your child with a safe space to express their feelings and give them tools to cope with the stress. Therapy can be especially helpful if your child is showing signs of anxiety, depression, or behavioral issues. It's important to address emotional concerns early on so they don't develop into more significant challenges later.

Taking Care of Your Own Emotional Well-Being

While your child's well-being is paramount, don't forget about your own emotional health. The custody battle can be exhausting, and it's easy to overlook your own needs during the process. However, taking care of yourself is just as important because your emotional state directly impacts how you can support your child. Here are some strategies for prioritizing your emotional well-being:

1. Practice Self-Care

Make time for yourself, even during the most hectic times, taking a walk, reading a book, or spending time with friends. Self-care can help you recharge and manage stress.

2. Seek Emotional Support

Surround yourself with supportive friends, family, or a counselor who can offer a listening ear and advice. The emotional toll of a custody battle can be heavy, and having someone to talk to can help you process your feelings and make decisions from a place of clarity.

3. Stay Organized and Focused

The more organized you are, the less stressed you will feel. Create a plan to keep track of important dates, documents, and tasks related to the custody battle. This will help reduce feelings of overwhelm and give you a sense of control over the situation.

Strategic Suggestions

- **Monitor Emotional Signs:** Keep an eye on your child's behavior. Changes in eating, sleeping, or school performance might be signs that they need extra emotional support.
- **Balance Focus:** While it's essential to support your child, remember to give yourself the emotional space you need to stay grounded. A calm parent can better help a struggling child.
- **Encourage Healthy Outlets:** Encourage your child to engage in hobbies or activities that they enjoy, such as sports or arts, to help relieve stress.
- **Revisit Conversations:** Sometimes, children need multiple conversations to fully process their feelings. Check in with

your child regularly to see how they are coping.

Prioritize your child's emotional health and managing your own to help navigate this difficult time with resilience and understanding. Both of you can emerge from this experience with stronger emotional well-being and a closer, more supportive relationship.

Maintaining Consistent Parenting Practices

During a custody battle, one of the most important things you can do as a father is maintain consistency in your parenting practices. Children thrive on routine and stability, especially when there are significant changes in their lives. The ongoing custody process can lead to a lot of uncertainty for your child, and the best way to counteract this uncertainty is by providing a strong foundation at home, no matter where your child is staying.

Why Consistency is Important

Consistency in parenting helps create a sense of security for your child, which is especially important during challenging times like a custody battle. Children, particularly younger ones, often feel confused and stressed when they are bounced between two different parenting styles, environments, or routines. Inconsistent discipline or a lack of structure can lead to feelings of anxiety and make it harder for your child to adjust.

In addition, consistent parenting reinforces positive behavior and helps your child understand what is expected of them. When your child experiences consistent boundaries and responses to their actions, they feel more confident and secure, knowing what to expect from you.

How to Maintain Consistent Parenting Practices

1. Establish Clear Boundaries

Consistent discipline is vital in helping your child understand the limits of acceptable behavior. When both parents maintain similar rules, it reduces confusion for the child. Ensure that you have established clear boundaries regarding things like screen time, bedtime, chores, and behavior. Even if you and your co-parent are living in separate homes, it's important to communicate and try to keep expectations aligned.

For example, if your co-parent limits screen time to two hours per day, try to follow a similar rule in your own home. If there are issues where you and your co-parent disagree, try to address them privately and come to an agreement. Children do better when they know the rules are the same at both homes.

2. Maintain Routines and Schedules

Kids thrive on routines, and during a custody battle, maintaining regular schedules can help your child feel more stable. As much as possible, try to keep your child's schedule consistent between both households. This includes regular bedtime routines, meal times, and time for homework or play. Keeping a routine can help your child adjust more easily to the changes and feel a sense of normalcy in an otherwise chaotic situation.

For example, if your child is used to going to bed at 8 p.m., try to keep that same bedtime when they are with you. If they are used to certain activities, such as family movie nights or weekend outings, continue those traditions to offer a sense of comfort.

3. Ensure Emotional Consistency

Emotional consistency means providing a steady, predictable source of support for your child. This can include offering comfort when they're upset, being available to talk about their feelings, and showing affection in ways they understand. When children feel loved and secure emotionally, they can better cope with the stress of the custody process.

Show your child that you are present and willing to listen. This helps them feel less anxious and more confident that their emotional needs will always be met.

4. Work on Effective Communication with Your Co-Parent

One of the most critical factors in maintaining consistency in parenting is good communication with your co-parent. While you may not agree on everything, it is essential to collaborate on matters relating to your child's well-being. Clear communication allows both parents to stay on the same page about the child's needs, behavior, and the logistics of custody arrangements.

This might mean regularly updating your co-parent on how your child is doing, discussing any changes to schedules, or even talking about how to handle particular situations, such as a recent tantrum or behavioral issue. Being open and communicative can help avoid any misunderstandings and ensure that both of you are reinforcing the same expectations.

5. Support Positive Behavior with Consistent Reinforcement

When your child behaves in ways that align with the boundaries and values you've established, it's important to acknowledge and reinforce that behavior. Praise, positive reinforcement, and even small rewards can go a long way in encouraging good behavior and ensuring your child feels confident and secure.

For example, if your child follows the rules and completes their homework, acknowledge their efforts with praise or a small reward, such as extra playtime or a treat. Consistent reinforcement of positive behavior helps your child understand that good actions lead to positive outcomes and helps them internalize the values you want to instill.

6. Be Predictable in Your Responses

As a parent, your responses to your child's behavior should be predictable, fair, and consistent. This means not overreacting in moments of frustration but instead taking a calm, measured approach. Children feel more secure when they know how you will respond to their actions.

Managing Difficult Situations with Consistent Parenting

While maintaining consistency can be challenging during a custody battle, it is still possible to handle difficult situations with a balanced approach. If you find that certain challenges or disagreements arise, keep these strategies in mind:

1. Don't Use Your Child as a Messenger

Avoid placing your child in the middle of any disputes with your co-parent. Do not use them as a messenger to pass along information or opinions about the custody process. This can create unnecessary stress for your child and may harm your relationship with them. It's important that you protect your child from any adult issues and let them focus on their own well-being.

2. Remain Calm During Disagreements

Disagreements are inevitable in any co-parenting arrangement, but it's important to remain calm and focused. If you feel upset or angry, take a moment to gather your thoughts before responding.

Strategic Suggestions

- **Keep a Parenting Journal:** Track the schedules, routines, and behaviors that you are maintaining consistently. This can help if you ever need to demonstrate to the court that you have been providing a stable and nurturing environment.

- **Stay Flexible:** While consistency is key, there will be times when you need to adjust. Be flexible and willing to adapt to your child's needs as they arise.
- **Collaborate with Your Co-Parent:** Communicate regularly to ensure that both households are aligned in terms of rules, expectations, and schedules. This cooperation demonstrates a commitment to putting your child's best interests first.

Maintain consistency in your parenting practices to provide your child with the stability and emotional support they need during a stressful time. Consistency will also help show the court that you are a responsible and reliable parent, strengthening your position in the custody battle.

Chapter 10: Finalizing Custody and Moving Forward

Finalizing custody and moving forward involves completing the legal process and transitioning into a stable routine for your family. This step is important for creating clarity and ensuring your child has a secure environment. Embracing this new phase with focus and positivity helps set the stage for a healthier future.

Understanding Custody Orders and Compliance

Once the court has made a decision about custody, you will receive a custody order. This order is a legal document that lays out the specific terms and conditions of your parental rights and responsibilities. Understanding this document is crucial because it dictates how you interact with your child, your ex, and how you must handle any future disagreements.

What Does a Custody Order Include?

A custody order typically includes several key details, including:

1. Physical Custody

This determines where your child will live and who will be responsible for day-to-day care. If you have joint physical custody, your child will spend significant time with both parents. If you have sole physical custody, your child will primarily live with you, and your ex may have visitation rights.

2. Legal Custody

This defines who has the right to make important decisions for your child, such as decisions about their education, healthcare, and religious upbringing. Joint legal custody means both parents share this responsibility, while sole legal custody means one parent has the right to make these decisions alone.

3. Visitation Schedules

The order may include a specific visitation schedule, detailing when the child will spend time with the non-custodial parent. This schedule will include weekends, holidays, school vacations, and other special days.

4. Child Support

If you are the non-custodial parent, the court will likely outline a child support arrangement, specifying how much you are required to pay for your child's care and expenses.

5. Special Conditions

Custody orders may also include additional conditions based on your specific circumstances. For example, there may be provisions related to supervised visitation or drug or alcohol testing.

Compliance with Custody Orders

Once you have the custody order, it's critical to follow it carefully. Failing to comply with the terms of the order could result in serious legal consequences, such as losing custody, paying fines, or being held in contempt of court.

Here are some steps to help you comply with your custody order:

1. Stay Organized

Keep a copy of the custody order in a safe and accessible place. Make sure you are clear about your responsibilities and dates. This includes visitation schedules, holidays, and important appointments for your child.

2. Respect the Schedule

If the court has set specific times for visitation or custody exchanges, follow them closely. If you need to make changes, such as requesting a different pick-up time, always try to communicate in advance and reach a mutual agreement with your ex.

3. Document Everything

If there are issues with visitation or custody arrangements, document everything. This includes missed visits, delays, or any issues with your child's well-being. Keeping a record of your actions shows you are following the court order and can protect you in case of future disputes.

4. Keep Communication Professional

The way you communicate with your ex will play a big role in maintaining compliance. It's important to stay civil and stick to the terms of the order. If you feel the need to discuss issues outside of the scheduled visitation, do so respectfully, and if necessary, involve your attorney.

5. Follow Child Support Guidelines

If you are required to pay child support, make sure you follow the payment schedule outlined in the custody order. If you face financial difficulties and cannot make payments, immediately contact the court or your attorney to seek modifications.

What to Do If There's a Violation

Situations may arise where your ex does not comply with the custody order. They may not allow you to visit your child at specific times or may refuse to follow the agreed-upon schedule. If this happens, here's what you can do:

1. Attempt Communication

If your ex is violating the order, try to communicate with them calmly. They may have misunderstood the order or could be going through a difficult time.

2. Request Mediation

Mediation can be a helpful tool in resolving custody disputes. A mediator can help both parties work toward a solution without having to go to court.

3. File a Motion for Contempt

If communication and mediation do not work, you may need to go back to court. If your ex is violating the custody order, you can file a motion for contempt. The court can then enforce the terms of the order, potentially with consequences for the non-compliant parent.

Strategic Suggestions

- Stay proactive in adhering to the custody order. It's easy to assume that once the order is made, everything will go smoothly, but keeping track of details and sticking to the schedule is key.

- Don't hesitate to seek legal help if there are uncertainties about the order or if you are facing difficulties complying.
- If you believe that modifications to the custody order are necessary, such as due to a change in your circumstances or your child's needs, consult with an attorney about filing a petition for modifications.

In conclusion, understanding and complying with your custody order is vital for maintaining your relationship with your child. Take it seriously, stay organized, and don't hesitate to seek help when necessary.

Preparing for Post-Judgment Modifications

Custody orders are designed to address the needs of your child at a specific time, but life circumstances often change. Children grow, and their needs evolve. Parents may experience changes in work, living conditions, or health. When significant changes occur after the court has issued the custody order, you may need to request modifications to the order.

When to Consider Modifying the Custody Order

Custody orders are not set in stone. They can be modified when there is a significant change in circumstances. Some common reasons that parents request a modification include:

1. Change in Living Situation

If you or your ex have moved to a new location, it can impact the current visitation and custody schedule. For example, if one parent moves far away, it may no longer be practical for the child to travel frequently between homes.

2. Change in Employment

If either you or your ex has a change in work hours or job location that affects your ability to care for the child or share custody, a modification might be necessary.

3. Child's Needs

As children grow older, their emotional, physical, and educational needs change. A custody schedule that worked when the child was younger may no longer suit their needs. A child might also need additional care, such as if they develop a health condition or need special schooling.

4. Parental Health

If one parent experiences a health condition that makes it difficult for them to care for the child, this can be grounds for modifying the custody order. Similarly, if a parent's health improves or stabilizes, they may request additional custody time.

5. Substance Abuse or Abuse Allegations

If there are concerns regarding abuse, substance abuse, or neglect, either parent can petition the court for a modification. In such cases, the safety of the child is the most important factor for the court's consideration.

How to Request a Modification

The process of modifying a custody order involves filing a petition with the court that issued the original order. Here's how you can prepare for a modification request:

1. Consult with an Attorney

Before filing for a modification, it's crucial to speak with an experienced custody attorney. Your attorney will help assess if the changes in your circumstances qualify for a modification. They will guide you through the legal process, ensuring all requirements are met and that your petition is appropriately filed.

2. Document Changes in Circumstances

To prove that there's been a significant change in circumstances, you will need to provide evidence. This could include medical records, job changes, school records, or any other documentation that supports your claim. Keep a detailed record of any events or issues that may influence the child's best interests.

3. Ensure the Child's Best Interests

Remember that the court's primary concern is always the child's best interests. You will need to show that the proposed modification will benefit your child. For example, if you are requesting more time with your child, you must demonstrate how that time would improve their emotional or developmental well-being.

4. File the Petition

Once you have consulted with your attorney and gathered the necessary documentation, your attorney will file a petition for modification with the court. This petition will request a modification of the custody order based on the changes you've documented.

5. Prepare for the Court Hearing

Once your petition is filed, the court will schedule a hearing. During this hearing, you and your attorney will present evidence that supports your request for modification. Be prepared to explain the changes in your circumstances and how they impact the child's well-being. The judge may also hear from the other parent and any relevant witnesses before making a decision.

What to Expect in the Court Process

The court process for modifying a custody order can be lengthy. Here's what you can expect:

1. Mediation

Some courts require mediation before a hearing. Mediation is a process where a neutral third party helps both parents come to an agreement on custody modifications. If you and your ex can reach an agreement during mediation, the judge will likely approve the change without a formal hearing. However, if an agreement cannot be reached, the case will proceed to a hearing.

2. Court Hearing

If the case goes to a hearing, you and your ex will present your arguments to the judge. The judge will consider the evidence, including any changes in circumstances, and will decide if the proposed modification is in the best interests of the child.

3. Judge's Decision

After the hearing, the judge will issue a decision. If the judge grants the modification, the custody order will be adjusted accordingly. If the judge denies the modification, the current custody arrangement will remain in place.

Strategic Suggestions

- Be proactive in documenting any changes that may affect custody. Keeping a detailed record of significant life events can help you make a stronger case for a modification.

- Keep communication open with your ex. If possible, try to work out any changes amicably to avoid the need for a formal court process.
- Consult with an attorney to ensure that your modification request is legally sound. A knowledgeable attorney can help you navigate the complexities of the legal system and ensure that your request is presented effectively.

In conclusion, preparing for post-judgment modifications is a critical step in maintaining a custody arrangement that supports your child's well-being and accommodates changes in your life. Always prioritize your child's best interests, and work with legal professionals to ensure that any modifications are handled properly.

Co-Parenting Strategies for Long-Term Success

Co-parenting can be challenging, especially after a custody battle. However, creating a stable, cooperative environment for your child is one of the most important aspects of their well-being. Successful co-parenting is about putting aside personal differences and focusing on your child's needs. This can be difficult, but with the right strategies, you can develop a positive co-parenting relationship with your ex, which benefits everyone involved.

The Key to Successful Co-Parenting

Successful co-parenting starts with good communication. Even if your relationship with your ex is strained, it's crucial to keep lines of communication open and respectful. Both of you share the responsibility of raising your child, and your child deserves to have both parents actively involved in their life. Here are several strategies to help ensure your co-parenting relationship remains effective in the long term:

1. Establish Clear and Consistent Communication

One of the biggest challenges in co-parenting is managing communication effectively. It is vital to set up clear and consistent communication with your ex to avoid misunderstandings that can lead to conflicts. This means using respectful, calm language and focusing on your child's needs.

- **Set boundaries:** Agree on communication methods and frequency. Some parents find it useful to communicate only through email or a shared parenting app to keep things professional and organized.
- **Be direct and clear:** Keep your messages focused on the child's needs. If you need to discuss scheduling, medical

appointments, or school events, make sure you convey the information clearly.

- **Avoid using your child as a messenger:** Your child should not be put in the position of delivering messages between parents. This can create unnecessary stress for them and complicate their relationship with both of you.

2. Stick to the Custody Agreement

While life changes, and circumstances may require flexibility, it's important to follow the custody agreement as much as possible. Consistency is key in helping your child feel secure. This includes adhering to the visitation schedule, maintaining rules at both homes, and sticking to the agreed-upon arrangements unless a change is absolutely necessary.

If adjustments need to be made to the custody schedule, discuss it with your ex calmly, and be open to compromise when possible. If significant changes are needed, consult with a lawyer to ensure that any modifications are legally appropriate and protect your rights.

3. Create a Parenting Plan That Works for Both of You

A clear, mutually agreed-upon parenting plan provides structure and guidelines for your co-parenting relationship. Your plan should cover day-to-day decisions such as the child's school, medical care, and extracurricular activities, as well as long-term decisions like vacations, holidays, and special events.

When creating a parenting plan, make sure it's flexible enough to accommodate unforeseen changes.

- **Stay on the same page:** Ensure that both you and your ex have the same expectations for your child's routine, including bedtime, meals, and discipline.
- **Keep your child's needs in mind:** As your child grows, their needs will change.

You may need to revisit and adjust the plan to suit their evolving developmental and emotional needs.

4. Put Your Child's Needs First

One of the most important aspects of successful co-parenting is always prioritizing your child's emotional and psychological well-being. Children can sense conflict between their parents, and seeing you and your ex disagree can cause them stress and anxiety. Always keep their feelings in mind and try to maintain a united front, even if you disagree about something.

- **Work together on decisions:** As regards school choices or medical care, it's crucial that you and your ex are on the same page and make decisions that are best for your child.
- **Don't argue in front of your child:** Never use your child as a sounding board or argue with your ex in front of them.

This can cause confusion and emotional distress for your child, making them feel like they are caught in the middle.

Support your child's relationship with the other parent: Encourage your child to have a strong and healthy relationship with both parents. It's important for your child to feel they are equally loved and supported by both of you.

5. Focus on Positive Reinforcement

Children thrive on positive reinforcement, so always praise your child when they behave well, and celebrate their achievements. This helps them feel good about themselves and reinforces positive behavior. It's also important to offer praise to your ex when they make positive contributions to the child's life, fostering goodwill and cooperation.

- **Acknowledge the good:** When your ex makes an effort in the co-parenting relationship, acknowledge it. This can help build mutual respect and reduce tension.

- **Be patient and forgiving:** Co-parenting requires patience. Both you and your ex may make mistakes or face difficult times. Be willing to forgive, let go of resentment, and focus on the long-term goal: your child's happiness and security.

6. Respect Each Other's Roles

Co-parenting is about balancing two households, and each parent plays a crucial role in their child's life. Respecting each other's parenting style, home, and role is essential. Even if you disagree with your ex on how to handle certain issues, try to be respectful and understanding of their role in your child's upbringing.

- **Avoid criticizing your ex:** Negative comments or criticisms about the other parent can damage the child's perception of them. Even if you're frustrated, it's best to handle those feelings privately and not in front of your child.

- **Provide equal opportunities:** Ensure that both you and your ex have equal opportunities to spend quality time with your child, even if your schedules are different.

Strategic Suggestions

- Use a parenting app to track custody schedules, school events, and medical appointments. This can help keep both you and your ex organized and on the same page.
- If tensions are high, consider seeking mediation. A neutral third party can help both parents resolve conflicts and build a stronger co-parenting relationship.
- Be proactive in maintaining a respectful and patient approach. If issues arise, address them calmly, and don't let resentment build over time.

In conclusion, successful co-parenting requires effort, communication, and a commitment to putting your child's needs first. Stay organized, focused on your child's well-being, and respectful toward your ex, so you can build a strong, positive co-parenting relationship that provides stability and security for your child in the long term.

Conclusion

As you reach the final page of this book, take a moment to reflect on everything you've gained. ***LegalWay's Winning Child Custody Battle for Fathers*** was crafted to guide you through every step of the custody process. From understanding the law to building a strong case, navigating court procedures, and supporting your child, this book has armed you with the tools and knowledge needed to advocate for your role as a father.

The journey doesn't end here. The real work lies in applying what you've learned to your unique circumstances. The strategies and advice presented in these chapters are most effective when you take the time to personalize them to your situation. Revisit sections as needed, use the checklists and tips to stay organized, and lean on the wisdom shared to make informed decisions.

To get the most out of this resource, stay proactive. Knowledge is power, but action is what turns that power into results. Organize your paperwork meticulously, practice your communication skills, and remain focused on your child's best interests at all times. Keep the principles you've learned here in mind as you move forward. Consistency, patience, and preparation will continue to be your strongest allies.

Don't hesitate to seek additional support where needed, whether it's through legal professionals, trusted mentors, or co-parenting counselors. Combine the insights from this book with expert guidance, and you'll be even better positioned to navigate any challenges that arise.

If you've found this book helpful, consider leaving a review to share your thoughts. Reviews are invaluable not only to the author but also to other fathers who might be facing the same struggles you once did. Your feedback could inspire someone else to take the crucial first step toward advocating for their child.

Additionally, check out other related books by the author. Each offers unique insights and strategies tailored to various aspects of family law, parenting, and self-improvement. Whether you're looking for advice on co-parenting, handling post-judgment modifications, or improving communication with your child, these resources can provide further support.

As you close this chapter and look ahead, remember that being a father is one of the most rewarding roles in life. Your commitment to your child and your willingness to fight for them speak volumes about your character and love. This process isn't just about winning a case; it's about showing your child what it means to be resilient, determined, and unwavering in your care.

Take a deep breath, stay focused, and keep moving forward. You have what it takes to build a brighter future—not just for yourself, but for the person who matters most: your child.

www.ingramcontent.com/pod-product-compliance
Lightning Source LLC
Chambersburg PA
CBHW052143220526
45471CB00004B/1498